"*Miscarried Hope* is the book I wish I had as I stumbled through my own messy journey of loss. Using the events of Holy Week as a backdrop, Rachel is masterful in walking us through her brilliant framework: the Five Stages of Hope. As a marriage and family therapist, I will use this as my go-to resource for individuals and couples who have encountered the pain of pregnancy and infant loss. As a mom who has lost five babies to miscarriage, I will keep this book on my own nightstand and pass it to friends who share this pain too. As you read, take your time—there's a fount of comfort and truth on every page!"

Nicole Zasowski, marriage and family therapist and author of *What If It's Wonderful?*

"When I unexpectedly miscarried my sweet baby, grief filled the empty space that my baby was supposed to be growing in. As a pastor, I have counseled numerous women who have walked through loss. Yet, when I personally experienced the unthinkable, I was left to sort through so many questions. That is why this book is a must!

It is a gift for anyone who has experienced the loss of a child or anyone who may be walking with a friend or family member who has experienced loss. Rachel invites the broken to have a seat and know they are seen, known, and not alone. Beautifully written, Rachel does a stunning job of pulling us closer to Jesus and stirring our hearts."

Nicole Lynn Rowan, minister, mentor, and mom

"I've heard about the stages of grief before, but this is the first time I've heard about the stages of hope. What a beautiful concept to rest a heart on. Rachel has an incredible way of articulating the reality of the profound grief that ensues from miscarriage, stillbirth, and infant loss alongside the reality of a hope that, no matter how distant it can appear, still remains. She writes about both without diminishing either, giving every loss mom the ability to see herself in the pages of this book. W
heartbreaking loss, confusion, an

give us a glimpse of ourselves through the lens of God's promises and buoyant hope. What a gift."

Jessica Latshaw, musician, writer, and cohost of *The TJ [& Jess] Show* podcast

"Miscarrying my baby was the first significant death I had encountered in my life. Disoriented in my grief, I asked all the questions: Why had this happened, who could understand this pain, and how was I to process this as a praying woman? Rachel Lohman has written the book I wish I'd had on hand, naming the losses with tenderness and taking our hands as Jesus does to gently map the anatomy of both grief and hope."

Bronwyn Lea, loss mom and author of *Beyond Awkward Side Hugs*

"*Miscarried Hope* is the book I wish someone had put in my hands when I lost my baby as a result of miscarriage. It's packed full of comfort, truth, and, of course, hope. Rachel's voice is a wise and tender guide, ultimately pointing us toward Christ, speaking words of life on every page."

Ruthie Kim, executive coach and founder of Because Justice Matters

"As a fellow loss mom, I was eager to read Rachel's book. Void of trite phrases and empty words, *Miscarried Hope*'s refreshing perspective fills a gap between the church and women who are aching to explore their faith through the lens of grief. Bring your doubts, fears, and questions, and allow Rachel to be your guide on the journey toward a stronger faith and a renewed hope."

Peyton Lauderdale, cofounder of Gathering Hope

"By vulnerably sharing her story of loss, Rachel reminds the reader that even in our most difficult trials, Jesus is with us. She avoids trite answers and empty faith but offers a biblical perspective of hope and trust that is so needed in the body today. I wholeheartedly endorse this message."

Lee M. Cummings, founding and senior pastor at Radiant Church and author of *School of the Spirit* and *Flourish*

"*Miscarried Hope* is an insightful, heartfelt journey through grief and heartache and toward hope and transformation. No doubt you are glancing at this book because of pain in your life or the life of someone you love. Rachel Lohman is the friend from afar and the guide you want at your side in this moment. She is centered, authentic, kind, and filled with rich insight from her own paths of pain and spiritual anchoring. Let her bless you and help you through these pages."

Craig Springer, vice president at Barna Group and author of *How to Follow Jesus* and *How to Revive Evangelism*

"*Miscarried Hope* invited me on a gentle journey toward healing. As a mom who has experienced loss, I've lacked language for my pain. Now I have the words."

Sandy Wickham, colead pastor at Park Hill Church

"*Miscarried Hope* describes the loss of a child through miscarriage, still birth, or infant loss as 'wandering in a wilderness or a desert place.' Surviving the pain is a huge challenge both for individuals and for couples. For those who are suffering, Rachel's book is like drinking a draught of cool water. Taking inspiration from Jesus's journey from Palm Sunday to Resurrection Sunday, Rachel gives a road map for traveling that desert road with a guide who has been there before us. She shows how Jesus's compassion and love can bring healing and fresh hope.

Miscarried Hope is a wonderful resource, not only for any woman who has experienced the trauma of losing a child but also for couples seeking to understand how to support each other as they walk through this dark valley. Rachel points to Jesus every step of the way as the Shepherd who will refresh and restore our souls."

Nicky and Sila Lee, founders of The Marriage Course and authors of *The Marriage Book*

"I wish I had this book when we lost our baby. It is such a gift to have someone put into words the horror and grief it is to walk through such heartbreaking loss, but greater is the gift of hope.

What a gift to have a friend like Rachel hold our hands as we wrestle, doubt, grieve, and come around to hope once again—hope that is a person and hope that draws near and holds us.

I am so grateful for Rachel's courage and truth that shine a beacon of light for all of us who have walked through miscarriage."

Alyssa Bethke, cofounder of Family Teams and author of *Satisfied* and *Love that Lasts*

Miscarried Hope

Journeying with Jesus through Pregnancy and Infant Loss

Rachel Lohman

Revell

a division of Baker Publishing Group
Grand Rapids, Michigan

Published by Revell
a division of Baker Publishing Group
Grand Rapids, Michigan
www.revellbooks.com

Printed in the United States of America

Library of Congress Cataloging-in-Publication Data
Names: Lohman, Rachel, 1988– author.
Title: Miscarried hope : journeying with Jesus through pregnancy and infant loss / Rachel Lohman.
Description: Grand Rapids, Michigan : Revell, a division of Baker Publishing Group, [2023] | Includes bibliographical references.
Identifiers: LCCN 2022056679 | ISBN 9780800743000 (paperback) | ISBN 9780800745127 (casebound) | ISBN 9781493443581 (ebook)
Subjects: LCSH: Children—Death—Religious aspects—Christianity. | Miscarriage—Religious aspects—Christianity. | Miscarriage—Anecdotes. | Grief—Religious aspects—Christianity. | Hope—Religious aspects—Christianity. | Holy week.
Classification: LCC BV4907 .L65 2023 | DDC 248.8/66—dc23/eng/20230221
LC record available at https://lccn.loc.gov/2022056679

The author is represented by the literary agency of Credo Communications, LLC, www.credocommunications.net.

Some names and details have been changed to protect the privacy of the individuals involved.

Baker Publishing Group publications use paper produced from sustainable forestry practices and post-consumer waste whenever possible.

23   24   25   26   27   28   29   7   6   5   4   3   2   1

To my first child:
Because of your life and death,
I experience motherhood, hope,
and Jesus more fully each day.
Your life has changed mine.

I love you and miss you.

Contents

Introduction

If you're reading these words, I'm sorry. *Deeply* sorry.

You have this book in your hands most likely because you or someone close to you experienced pregnancy or infant loss. I wish this wasn't a road we would need to walk together.

But I'm also deeply thankful that we get to walk this road hand in hand. Why? Because while pregnancy or infant loss can be an isolating journey, one with more questions than answers, it is a journey that *changes* you.

After my loss, people told me about the stages of grief, but nobody told me that hope has stages too. I'm eager to share with you what I've coined as the Five Stages of Hope: expectation, shock, despair, grief, and active hope. Using the events of Holy Week as a backdrop, we'll see how Jesus and his followers walked amid these five stages and how naming these stages can radically inform our journeys after loss. Within these pages are also excerpts from the real, raw stories of fellow loss moms, as well as new research from four hundred loss moms I polled. Their stories are built into the bones of this book.

This is not a book of Band-Aids. You will not find clichés, platitudes, or silver linings attempting to soothe your wound. A baby dying is not a surface-level cut a mother can ever patch. It's a wound that lives deep in the heart, for which I believe resurrected hope to be the only balm. This book will also not attempt to answer the "why" questions behind your baby's death. I was convinced that having those answers would heal my heart after my miscarriage, but in hindsight, what I really needed was presence—God's presence. I needed to know I wasn't alone in my experience; I needed concrete assurance that the creator of the universe was with me and understood my hurt.

So, what you'll find in this book is just that: a trusted hand to hold, a road map for this confusing type of grief I quickly realized people don't talk about, and a place to honestly wrestle with God. And speaking of honesty, I want to remind you before we go a page farther that it is okay to struggle with your faith after loss. It is okay to have trust issues with hope—and with God. You *will* find hope again. Much to my own surprise, the hope I found after loss was more beautiful, deeper, and more transforming than I imagined was possible.

I'm here to gently take you by the hand now and walk with you as you discover this for yourself.

one

A Two-Thousand-Year-Old Road Map

I knew this was both birth and death happening at once. How do you wrap your brain around that?

Holly, loss mom

I had all kinds of feelings but no road map for what to do with them. And they were not the kinds of pleasant feelings you can delve into when acquaintances ask how you're doing; these were the kinds of feelings that are too muddled together to name and are even heavier to carry. The feelings that, when shared with the listening world, are met with silent stares from people unable to grasp the complexity of your pain. They're only able to fumble out "I can't imagine" in response. Where, then, do these feelings go? They get stuffed even deeper inside, under the belief that they must really be too much. I had a list of running questions that got longer each day, but I had no place to find answers. I had gone to the sources I knew—my doctor, my church, my friends, and God—but no answers could satisfy. My baby had died, but as the months progressed, I started realizing that other things had died too.

I miscarried a lot along with my baby: my blissful expectations of motherhood, my innocent optimism, my dreams for beginning a family, my relatively uncomplicated relationship with God, and my trust in my body, to name a few. But there was something more I lost. It was like a thin thread, almost too hard to pinpoint, undergirding all of these feelings, questions, and losses. It felt like the puzzle piece you can't locate, yet you also can't make sense of the full picture until you find it. But one day I did. I realized I had miscarried hope.

Through my work with Hope Again Collective, a handmade earring line I began in the hallway of my house in 2020, I've had the deep honor of walking alongside hundreds of women who have also experienced infant loss. Each earring I make bears the name of a fellow loss mom and shares her story. And every pair sold provides practical grief resources after a mom loses her baby. Like your experience, the backgrounds of these moms and the unique particulars surrounding their losses are different—but our stories share one common thread: a miscarriage of *hope*.

You can't live without hope. But most of us go through life without a conscious awareness that we are living *with* hope, that hope is propelling us into tomorrow. Hope is one of those things you don't realize you have—or had—until it feels like you've lost it.

Once you've experienced pregnancy loss or infant loss, your relationship with hope is never the same. Grieving the innocence of the hope you once had is tacked onto the list of secondary losses after your baby dies. Under the enormous weight of grieving the death of your baby, you're grieving what feels like a loss of hope. You're grieving a changed relationship with hope. And all the while, you're making fragile negotiations with hope to return to your heart where it so naturally dwelled before your world turned upside down.

I'm convinced that miscarriage and stillbirth grief is one of the most unique forms of grief a person can experience, for reasons we will continue to name as we journey together. Society, with all of its modern adaptations and technological advances, even with its progressions in women's rights and mental health awareness, is still years behind in how to address and care for loss moms. Where can you go with all of your questions, feelings, doubts, thoughts, anger, and grief? Where can you find validation for your experience without the shame or silence of others? Where can your soul breathe its heaviest sighs of disappointment and anger and questions to God? Where can you even begin to find the road back to hope again?

Here.

Right here.

These pages are for you—to serve as the road map back to hope you've been searching for. This road map is not precise and scientific with boxes to check and stages to reach. Instead, it is real and honest, and it looks a bit like those beautiful sidewalks in old neighborhoods with tree roots causing unexpected ups and downs in the pavement. There have been bumps in your loss journey already, and there will be more bumps in your grief ahead. For me, this journey back to hope is forged in the fire of my personal pain and is solidified by the thousands of loss moms I've walked with in the years since my baby died. Your experience can find home here.

You may be skeptically wondering how it is even possible to mutter the word *hope* or fantasize about a future with hope in it as you stare deep pain in the face now. After my baby died, I desperately needed to know that hope would one day return to my vocabulary. I even remember feeling selfish for wanting hope again, yet I couldn't shake the desire. In the lonely depths of fresh grief, I yearned to know that a restored relationship with God, restored confidence in my body, and a restored ability to dream about a new motherhood journey would be possible. If you share these desires now, let me reassure you that they are normal—and not selfish. Desiring future hope in no way diminishes the grief of your baby dying.

So how is hope even possible after surviving a miscarriage or stillbirth? I have found the answer lies in one name—Jesus. And I'm not just giving you a Sunday school answer. I've *only* found hope again because of Jesus. And it took me awhile. You may be angry at God right now and full of questions; you might be doubting your faith or trying to reconcile how a good God could allow your baby to die. These feelings aren't bad; they are an invitation. I invite you to recognize them, name them, and allow yourself to wrestle with them as they arise. Your feelings don't just matter right now; they will also play a significant role in how your unique grief process unfolds ahead.

Life Is Not Supposed to Be like This

Let's begin this journey together by addressing some of those elephants-in-your-mind types of feelings:

> Your baby dying is *really* unfair.
>
> This experience *sucks*.
>
> Your life is not supposed to be like *this*.

Go ahead—you have permission to replace *your* with *my* and say those phrases out loud. I don't want to start by telling you about the unique details of my baby dying—though we'll get there—because I know that if your journey through loss was anything like mine, you had very few people, if any, address these awkward and complicated feelings. What kept me awake at night were swirling thoughts of unfairness and this confusing sense that I didn't know quite how to reconcile. I knew my pregnancy experience was not supposed to be like this. Deep down you may have an inkling of this truth, and perhaps that inkling is what adds a layer of confusion to your feelings over your baby dying.

Babies are not supposed to die prematurely, before they can be held in Mom's and Dad's arms and grow into toddling children who chase bubbles and butterflies. Parents are not supposed to bury children in the ground before they're buried in middle school homework. Moms are *supposed* to watch their sons round the bases at humid summer T-ball games and help their daughters try on wedding dresses. Pregnancy? That's *supposed* to be the easy, fun part, right? *"It will happen when you're ready!" "You'll glow!"*

"Motherhood will be your best adventure yet!" Bodies are not supposed to bleed the painful aches of death from within. Hearts aren't meant to break this way. Dreams aren't meant to be crushed into a thousand little pieces that seem to fracture life altogether. Parenthood isn't meant to be *this* devastating.

Amy, a mom who experienced multiple miscarriages, shared with me: "When the doctor told me 'no heartbeat' for a second time, I felt like the floor was falling out underneath me. Was this some kind of cruel joke to have two miscarriages in six months? This isn't the way it's supposed to be. Two pregnancies. No babies to hold."

Life is not supposed to be like *this*.

Motherhood is not supposed to be like *this*.

And it's perfectly normal if the reality of that truth makes you want to scream. It's okay if it spins you into a thousand questions of why. You don't have to be religious or follow Jesus to have an innate sense that life is not supposed to be this painful. In fact, I see the same justice-soaked rage in agnostic moms who have shared their stories with me as I do in moms who have devoted their lives to Jesus. We know we are created for life. We know death is the enemy. This knowing is deeply laid into the heart of humanity, which is precisely why pregnancy and infant loss feel like an obnoxious punctuation of this truth. Why would bringing life into the world, something natural and beautiful, instead become a very personal source of death? This reality is emphasized when you experience a miscarriage, a stillbirth, or your living baby dies. It feels so unfair.

We live in a culture that tells women a large percentage of their worth and contribution to society comes from the children they produce. What do we do when the opportunity to earn that cultural badge is taken from us, when we feel like we didn't even get a fair chance? How do we process the unfair reality that some women have kids but didn't want them, got pregnant with minimal effort, or see motherhood only as a burden? Meanwhile you and I have waited to become moms, have wanted to become moms, and would be devoted moms. We don't say these things aloud, because they sound horrible, but we think them. We're met again and again with the stinging reality of how unfair pregnancy and infant loss feel when the joyful ease into motherhood is snatched from our hands. Surely life wasn't supposed to be like this, right?

But because we experience life on earth that is infused with pains and injustices and premature death, how do we make sense of our suffering? How do we have real hope and not fairy-tale naivety? Will all of the brokenness we experience *actually* be redeemed? How do we believe God can be good and in control when unfair suffering like pregnancy and infant loss have been part of our experiences?

I thought my years of graduate theology work had given me enough studying to weather these questions and keep me believing that God was good even when I suffered. But in the months following the death of my baby, all certainties were erased. Everything I thought I knew about Jesus beyond a shadow of a doubt *became* a doubt. My confidences about who God is and what it means to live in relationship with him were all on the table, open for examination. I consulted every book I could find to help my doubts. Late-night Google searches became my best friend. I'm sure I annoyed my husband with philosophical conversations. I was so desperate to know why my life was filled with brokenness and pain if God was good, loving, and in control. I wrestled. I searched and worked to the bottom of my beliefs and quite honestly approached God many times, pleading, *Just show me who you really are. Show me what's true.*

There was something about taking the time to probe into this lingering truth emerging to my heart's surface—that life isn't supposed to be this way—that brought about a new freedom. Simply asking the hard questions and no longer shying my ugly feelings away from the only one who has the potential to satisfy my doubts was liberating. For the first time as a follower of Jesus and as a pastor, I stopped hiding behind optimism. I began questing for real truth, and pain was what put me there. In times of suffering, your beliefs rise to the surface, and they directly affect how you cope. There's a brilliant, retired pastor in New York City that I love, who has also experienced deep suffering. He writes this about suffering: "No one can function without some set of beliefs about it all."[1] What you believe about your baby dying—whether it is true or not—will largely shape the hope you carry and the woman you'll become after carrying this pain. What you believe about it all—your emotions, your questions, your doubts—matters.

The Original Garden

In the summer months after my baby died, my wrestling with God led me to revisit where all of this pain started. For the first time, I felt like I was starting to investigate my own beliefs about the world to make sense of the senselessness. I was led back to the beginning, to the very first book of the Bible, where some wild events took place.

In the book of Genesis, we read that God made a beautiful, perfect world teeming with fruitful creation—animals, sunrises, flowers, and human beings—and he called it all *good*. But God's perfect design for our world was shattered by the sin of the first humans, Adam and Eve, wanting to be God without God. (Please note: I am not now nor will I ever suggest your baby dying is a result of sin or you doing something wrong. If anyone tells you that, I'm sorry, and I suggest you run in the other direction.) After Adam and Eve ate the forbidden fruit—a culmination of believing lies from the serpent, which led to doubting God's promises—God asked them, "What is this you have done?" (3:13). You can actually hear the sorrow and disappointment in God's heart. With this, God's perfect design for life and creation was infected with sin.

Why does this matter to your experience? Because it's really important to know that miscarriage was not part of God's original design. Death was not part of God's *good* plan for his people. Yet because of what happened in the original garden with Adam and Eve, we face many forms of death today—from cancer to divorce to broken dreams to infant loss. Death is not just a person's last breath. Death is also the decay or breakdown of anything created to be *good* for human flourishing. God is a God of goodness, not an author of evil. He's a God of life, not death. All the good things you enjoy—from an unexpected sunset to laughter with loved ones to a delicious meal and, yes, even the elation you felt when you found out you were pregnant—are gifts from the goodness of God's hand. Heartache, illness, miscarriage, stillbirth, and all of the evil we experience while inhabiting a sin-stricken world are not given by God. Permitted, yes—due to the sin of humanity— but none of them were part of God's *original* plan for goodness. As one loss mom shared, "Knowing that God didn't want this for me helped me cope. God didn't take away my babies; that was sin. . . . God doesn't withhold good things from us, and he knows our needs better than we do. It is a difficult dichotomy to comprehend."[2]

So, what difference does this make to you now? Understanding the root of our world's brokenness can be a really helpful container to hold everything that doesn't make sense in the wake of your baby dying. Even if you aren't a Christian and don't fully believe how sin entered our world and the role it plays now, you can't deny that Genesis 3 offers an explanation for why you know in your bones that life isn't supposed to be this way.

If there is no root of sin and brokenness, how do we explain the evils of death, like pregnancy and infant loss? One loss mom shared, "I'm not religious. Although, after my loss, I wish I was so I could've turned to something." Thankfully, you can try out this understanding of sin and brokenness as the container for your questions and doubts. God lends it freely. And maybe you'll discover that this understanding can become the seed of hope for your future. Again, you don't need to desire hope now. But know that this little seed can be planted in the ground now, topped with messy dirt, and forgotten about as you do the watering work of walking the grief road from death to hope.

Friend, the pain you carry is not how your story will end. The story of God didn't end when Adam and Eve brought sin into the world. He didn't leave behind a broken world. He cared too much to *not* respond. And his response has your experience at the heart of it: God put a plan into motion to redeem everything that has experienced death. That includes your baby, your heart, your dreams of motherhood, your relationships, and even the hope that you'll see your baby again. The death you see now does not and will not have the last word. How can I be sure? Because two thousand years ago, during Holy Week, when the stakes were at their highest for God's rescue plan to prevail, death looked absolutely final.

And unexpectedly, hope arose.

Holy Week and the Five Stages of Hope

If you're unfamiliar with Holy Week, it is what Christians call the week leading up to the death, burial, and resurrection of Jesus (better known as the week between Palm Sunday and Easter). Holy Week is more than just a historical documentation of Jesus's final days on earth. It encapsulates more than just a few somber days before Easter dresses and egg hunts emerge. Holy Week chronicles the movement from death to hope.

And for a loss mom, I believe Holy Week is an extremely helpful paradigm to process the unique roller coaster of grief we experience as we see the hope of new life turn traumatically into death. Connecting my own story of miscarriage to Jesus's experiences during Holy Week, as well as to the Five Stages of Hope I believe find their origins in Holy Week, has single-handedly been the most helpful process for my personal hope and healing. Could it be that the road map for grief, healing, and hope after infant loss was already written over two thousand years ago?

- In the **expectation** of Jesus's triumphant Palm Sunday announcement, we as loss moms remember the expectation and anticipation of the positive pregnancy test.
- In the **shock** of the Last Supper, we as loss moms remember the shock of the first signs of miscarriage/stillbirth.
- In the **despair** of Good Friday, we as loss moms find a place for the lonely feeling of being forsaken by God when we needed him most.

- In the **grief** of Silent Saturday, we as loss moms sit in the feeling of time standing still as the storm of disbelief, disorientation, and deep disappointment swirled around us.
- And in the **active hope** of Resurrection Sunday, we as loss moms are invited into a real, living hope that we, too, will see our babies again, because of Jesus's miraculous defeat of death.

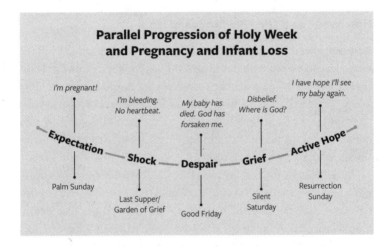

Parallel Progression of Holy Week and Pregnancy and Infant Loss

With all of your unanswered questions and big feelings in one hand, I invite you to open your other hand to the possibility of rediscovering hope for your story through what Holy Week and these Five Stages of Hope can offer you. While the events of Holy Week have beginning and end points, the Five Stages of Hope do *not*. They do not have clear transition points, and it's likely you will (and maybe already are) experiencing many of these stages simultaneously. Because the road to active hope is fluid, we'll explore these stages together in the same way—without particular start and end points, but rather as they naturally arise out of the events of Holy Week and the events of infant loss.

Life after pregnancy and infant loss is complex but not too complex for the God who made you and your baby. I've spent years wrestling my way through the implications of Holy Week on my miscarriage, and along the way, I discovered that Jesus isn't who I thought he was either. He was more familiar with grief and nearer in my pain than I knew. I pray that as we walk this road together, you'll meet Jesus in your grief in unexpected ways and discover firsthand that your miscarried hope can be resurrected too.

PART I
The Death of Friday

Stages of Hope:
Expectation and Shock

two

Great Expectations

I walked around completely swathed in this glowing cloud after finding out I was pregnant.

Taylor, loss mom

My mom had flown out for a long weekend to visit us in our new home. Our very first home as a married couple was just three miles from the ocean in Long Beach, California. After four failed attempts to buy a house in the previous year, our offer was chosen, and we were ecstatic. It was a gorgeous flip home with renewed interiors. It was painted a charming 1920s craftsman-style yellow with white trim and was a petite nine hundred square feet in total. The perfect starter home for my husband and me, this was the home we hoped to welcome children into. Unbeknownst to either of us, the weekend we spent hauling heavy boxes across town and up the porch steps into our new yellow house was the weekend my period was supposed to begin, but in the midst of moving chaos and speaking at a women's conference that weekend, I was too preoccupied to realize. The next week I had that exciting, curious moment of revelation. *Could I be pregnant?*

We stopped at a pharmacy on our way home from a long day at work, headed straight to the bathroom, and after thirty seconds that felt like an eternity of waiting for the pregnancy test to confirm or deny our dreams of entering parenthood, my husband and I burst into shouts when good news appeared on the tiny screen. At age twenty-nine, just shy of two years into marriage, our world was about to change forever. Sometimes you have those moments when it feels like heaven might be invading the earth you occupy. Like those dreams you've carried in your headspace for years are crashing into your reality. *Is this really happening? Is this too good to be true?*

The minute the pregnancy stick reads positive, expectations for the journey ahead begin to form. Even if you weren't planning to become pregnant or have mixed emotions about being pregnant, there's a part of the human heart that can't help but activate new dreams. Your due date becomes a special marker of the future, and expectations, anticipation, and excitement begin to grow in step with the life you now carry.

The Unexpected Step of Motherhood

When you're pregnant, for the first time especially, it can feel like you're carrying a fragile, invisible bubble in your hands. Nobody else can see it; nobody else knows the secret behind the added joy in your smile or the reason your eyes are sparkling a bit more with the anticipation of beholding a dream. This bubble can feel fragile. At least it did for me. But the possibility of this bubble being broken wasn't even on my radar. Pregnancy or infant loss had not happened to anyone close to me. Not one woman I knew personally had shared about their miscarriage with me; it was simply a sad statistic out there in the world, far away from me.

I always thought pregnancy and becoming a mom was one of the big boxes to check on the noble list of life's stages. The unspoken stairsteps of how life is *supposed* to unfold had structured my future dreams and hopes without anyone ever handing me a manual. This is the life that was modeled for me, or maybe this is the life that society deemed healthy and flourishing. And these were the steps I needed to climb.

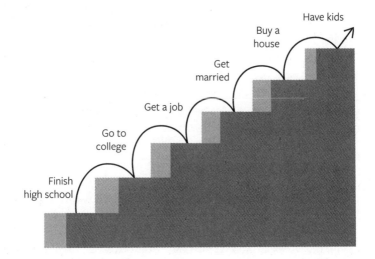

One of the many problems with the unspoken stairsteps of achievement for life is that motherhood (and all of these important milestones) becomes reduced to a box on a checklist, a season of life to anticipate without any expectation that pain just might be involved along the way. Motherhood becomes an achievement to attain, a status marker culture persuades women to believe is the pinnacle of their womanhood. But nobody talks about the suffering often required to climb from one step to the next, especially as women step into motherhood. At least nobody told me. The result? A naive, overly optimistic woman who was pregnant with new life and an unrealistic hope that this season would be all glow and no pain.

Our world expects women will desire motherhood, that women will naturally waltz into it with nothing but glow, that pregnancy happens easily, that staying pregnant happens easily, and that giving birth to a healthy, living baby happens easily. In an unbroken, unfallen world like the one God originally created, these expectations would be in touch with reality. But that is not the world we inhabit today. It is fallen, and pregnancies, bodies, and lives in general are subjected to pain and suffering and death, yet these roadblocks always catch us by surprise. So, what happens when these unrealistic expectations are unmatched to the reality we live in? When pain on the road to motherhood happens, from infertility to infant loss to postpartum depression and beyond, women experience the shock and grief of the unexpected. They feel isolated in their experience, their motherhood journey marginalized, and their hopes dashed. Loss is not what any of us expect when we first step into motherhood.

The Palm Sunday of Pregnancy

Palm Sunday marks the official start of Holy Week, and at its center is the triumphant entry of Jesus into Jerusalem as the long-awaited Messiah. If you've been to church on Palm Sunday, you've probably seen kids awkwardly and adorably waving around palm branches during the service. Palm Sunday is not simply a day of historical significance in the life of Jesus and his followers; it's rich with practical implications for us today, especially as loss moms. Because at its core, Palm Sunday is about high hopes and missed expectations.

Much of the story of God's people is about waiting for their promised Messiah—Jesus—to come onto the scene and fill that missing piece of the puzzle of God's redemption plan they had begun to piece together. Deep in the Scriptures was the promise that ancient Israel's future anointed king, the one who would rescue them, would come to his people in a royal procession riding a donkey (Zech. 9:9). In the ancient world, a donkey symbolized peace. To fulfill this promise, Jesus had his closest followers, known as his disciples, go ahead of him into the village and find a donkey. Here's what happened next:

> The disciples went and did as Jesus had instructed them. They
> brought the donkey and the colt and placed their cloaks on them

for Jesus to sit on. A very large crowd spread their cloaks on the road, while others cut branches from the trees and spread them on the road. The crowds that went ahead of him and those that followed shouted,

> "Hosanna to the Son of David!"
> "Blessed is he who comes in the name of the Lord!"
> "Hosanna in the highest heaven!"

When Jesus entered Jerusalem, the whole city was stirred and asked, "Who is this?" (Matt. 21:6–10)

Jesus chose a day of particular significance to ride in on a donkey. This day was the start of Jerusalem's annual festival known as Passover. Similar to how small towns throw Fourth of July parties with parades and fireworks today—but this was even more celebratory for Jerusalem. Hundreds of thousands of people would spend weeks making the hot, dusty pilgrimage through the desert to be in Jerusalem for the festival—all to celebrate the freedom they had received thousands of years earlier when God passed over Egypt. Passover Festival was the summer block party of all block parties—there was food, there was celebrating, and there were high anticipations that this *could* be the year God would deliver them from their Roman enemy.

And so, the people rallied. They lined the streets shouting "Hosanna," which literally means "come save us now."[1] Hosanna was the festival anthem, and Passover was the corporate stirring up of hope and pleading to God to send their Messiah and bring true, lasting freedom.

Maybe this would be the year that a long-awaited dream would come crashing into reality. Hopes held high, anticipations thick, expectations soaring.

Maybe this would be the cycle. Maybe this would be the positive pregnancy stick.

And to the people's surprise—it was. When Jesus came riding into the walls of the city's party, the parade route lined with palm branches, he fulfilled the ancient promise, confirming he was the long-awaited Messiah. Years upon years, generation after generation had been holding onto a strand of hope that their king would one day deliver his people—and the day had come! Yet this was not the king anyone *expected*. They expected a polished, warlike military figure with crushing strength and dogmatic authority, not a humble, lowly, donkey-riding Messiah. Their response captures the moment of missed expectation perfectly: "Who is this?" (21:10). They were confused and disappointed, the result of misaligned expectations. They wanted a conquering hero but instead came the Prince of Peace.

Expectations for God

It was not until my baby died that I was confronted head-on with my own expectations for Jesus. I entered into a confusing season of articulating and wrestling through the expectations I had formed for who God would be in my life and the dynamics of our relationship together. Just like the crowds on the side of the Jerusalem roads realized, through my loss it became disorienting yet clear that Jesus was not who I expected him to be.

In my humanness, I was not aware of the *years* I had spent building these spiritual expectations. There were certain things I expected from God and a certain type of life I expected as a result of following him. When I started to see the signs of miscarriage invading my pregnancy, my initial, instinctive expectation was that God would do a miracle. I pleaded with God, writing out my expectations in my journal:

I feel like I already had some questions, some doubts about you, God. Where are you as rescuer, as midcrisis miracle worker? Will I just know you cognitively in that way but never experience you in that way? Are miracles and divine interventions by your hand just for others? Am I limited to only experiencing some of who you are, God? What would you like me to tell the people I minister to about these parts of your character I have yet to actually know personally? Do I just smile and nod in agreement that you still do miracles on earth, even though you didn't for my baby? Will you show me firsthand these parts of who you claim to be? I want to believe it's true, God. I really do.

I expected God to stop my bleeding and keep our baby alive. Of course, he was capable. But God didn't save our child. My expectation was for a miracle on my command, and when my expectation wasn't met, I was angry, shocked, and disappointed—and not just for a few days. For months on end.

There are three common expectations I hear from women surrounding pregnancy, loss, and infertility. I've written these in such a way that you can clearly see the cause and effect, the logic behind why our pregnancy expectations are formed the way they are in our culture today. Which of these resonates with your journey?

- I expected pregnancy to happen easily *because* I haven't heard many firsthand stories of women struggling with infertility.
- I expected to have a healthy, normal pregnancy *because* I wasn't informed of how common miscarriage actually is and/or *because* I don't personally know anyone who has experienced miscarriage.
- I expected to deliver a healthy, living baby *because* there were no warning signs of stillbirth during my pregnancy and/or *because* I don't personally know anyone who has experienced stillbirth.

Let me affirm whichever of these expectations you resonate with. They are absolutely logical and rational. Even if you were aware of the possibility of pregnancy and infant loss, nobody expects to become the statistic. Out of the four hundred loss moms I surveyed, one-third said they feel guilty for not knowing their pregnancy could end in loss.

That's a lot of moms bearing the burden of guilt over a missed expectation.

This is one of the complications surrounding pregnancy and infant loss that breaks my heart. I hate that women are carrying guilt for not knowing about the possibility of infant loss, while our culture simultaneously silences the stories of miscarriage and stillbirth when women try to tell them. We talk a lot about prenatal vitamins and nursery designs but very little about the possibility that motherhood can be a bumpy, complicated ride. Nobody wants to scare pregnant women or squash their hope. But at the same time, silence around pregnancy and infant loss creates really damaging, unspoken expectations. Until pregnancy and infant loss are seen as commonly occurring realities that can affect any pregnant woman at any time, we will continue perpetually feeding the expectation that pregnancy will be easy, blissful, and uncomplicated.

Taylor, a loss mom whose pregnancy began with a "glowing cloud," had her world turned upside down when she encountered the unexpected.

> Days of bleeding went on. I ended up laboring at work and delivered our sweet baby in the teacher's lounge bathroom. I was "only" six or seven weeks along, so, no, there wasn't much to my baby. But there she was. I was woefully unprepared mentally, physically, emotionally, and spiritually for this moment. Why hadn't anyone told me about this part? Why didn't my doctor warn me or prepare me? It sounds stupid, but I simply didn't know.

God of Miracles?

When I look back on the critical moments of my life—the times when I desperately needed a miraculous intervention from God—I notice a similar theme: God seemed silent during times of desperation but would show up afterward. I've seen God make beautiful things in my life from crumbled pieces of shattered dreams and hopes I thought were incapable of amounting to anything ever again. God has redeemed a lot of hopelessness and brokenness in my heart. I have experienced him as redeemer firsthand.

But in the midst of the panic and fear of potentially losing my baby, I told God that I didn't care about experiencing him as redeemer again. Right then, I just wanted—desperately needed—to experience him as a God of miracles. I needed him to show off his sovereign strength and meet my miracle expectation. Surely, I knew he was capable.

In fact, God was my only hope for saving my baby. There was no person, no professional, no medical device or drug to turn to aside from God. I wanted him to save my baby, absolutely. And a part of me also wanted to know that he really *was* a God of miracles like the Scriptures say and other people have experienced firsthand. I longed to know God in this way myself.

In the days that followed my urgent pleas, my circumstances only grew worse. I never experienced God rushing in like a super-hero to save the night for me and my dying child. Instead, God seemed distant and absent. If I was honest, I was holding some ungrounded expectation that he would have spared me from this pain in the first place. I expected God to be a genie in a bottle and conform to *my* expectations. I expected God to do a miracle on my command and save my baby. I expected that I'd be given a pain-free entrance to motherhood like everyone else I knew.

None of my expectations were met.

In the years that have passed since my miscarriage, I can tell you firsthand that God has exceeded the expectations I had for him in my pre-loss days. I never really expected that one day I'd gain a small bit of purpose from my pain. I didn't expect that I'd have a divine hand to hold through my tears or that I'd experience some redemption in my story. I honestly believe that if God had just met my limited, small expectations of who I wanted him to be and what I wanted from motherhood, I would've missed so much of the transforming journey God was inviting me into.

Before loss, motherhood was just a stairstep for me to climb, the next natural season for my life. After loss, motherhood became an absolute miracle and gift I had significantly undervalued.

And for those spiritual expectations I had to confront, Jesus has proven to be better, nearer, kinder, and more powerful than I ever expected. Loss showed me that life with God isn't a clear-cut math equation where one plus one always equals two.

Jesus didn't fit the expectations placed on him on Palm Sunday or a few days later on the cross or later yet in the tomb. In peculiar fashion, Jesus exceeded them.

One of my favorite Bible scholars sums up the invitation of Palm Sunday:

> As we arrive at Jerusalem with Jesus, the question presses upon us. Are we going along for the trip in the hope that Jesus will fulfill some of our hopes and desires? Are we ready to sing a psalm of praise, but only as long as Jesus seems to be doing what we want? The long and dusty pilgrim way of our lives gives most of us plenty of time to sort out our motives for following Jesus in the first place. Are we ready not only to spread our cloaks on the road in front of him, to do the showy and flamboyant thing, but also now to follow him into trouble, controversy, trial and death?[2]

Friend, could Jesus still be good even when he doesn't meet your expectations? Is it possible that a suffering savior might be better than a genie in a bottle?

And is it possible, even now—in the face of your warranted disappointment and hurt—to wave your palm branches and declare him king of your heart?

These are the questions the earliest followers of Jesus would be faced with in the days ahead of them as Holy Week marched on. Nobody prepared them for what was to come after the anticipation stirred up on Palm Sunday. And certainly, nobody expected the way to true, everlasting life would come through death.

three

The Shock of a Supper

We held our babies one last time, with tears streaming down in an unfathomable amount of pain.

Bridget, mom to Brooks and Bryce, twins lost to TTTS

I internally struggled to keep the news that I was pregnant from my mom until she made her cross-country trek to visit us in California on Memorial Day weekend. I picked her up from the airport on a Thursday afternoon, heart racing with anticipation of telling her our big news. We were expecting a new life—and she was going to be a grandma for the first time! When we got back into town from the airport, I dropped her off for lunch with a friend and headed back to my office. As I walked by the bright turquoise walls toward my desk, an eerie feeling passed over me. I felt as though I audibly heard, *There is no longer life in you.*

As someone who struggles with worst-case-scenario fears from time to time, I chalked it up to my mind wanting to get the best of me and steal the joy of this exciting day. The excitement would climax just hours later when Mark and I would take my mom out to dinner and hand her a belated Mother's Day card bearing her new title—grandma.

But even then, I couldn't fully shake off that unsettling moment in my office; it was so distinct. Was this some sort of foreshadowing for what lay ahead? Was God trying to prepare my heart? Was he sending me a warning?

I proceeded with the day as planned. Certainly I'd be fine; my baby would be fine. I was just new at all of this, and sometimes excitement is masked as anxiety, right? When my mom opened her card, her reaction was everything. It brought out the emotions in me I hadn't let myself feel yet—the tears of real excitement and joy. There was something about sharing the news of our pregnancy that made it real. It was no longer the invisible bubble I carried. Now it had weight. Now it was real. Now the anticipation and the hopes were even higher.

There's a running debate in circles of moms about the best timing to make a pregnancy announcement. Traditionally, to "play it safe," most women wait until after their first trimester to announce their news publicly. And that's the same rule of thumb I thoughtlessly planned to follow. I'd announce when I passed the first trimester. Nobody knew I was pregnant except the two people closest to me—my husband and my mom. In hindsight, I wish that first trimester rule didn't exist, because it further complicated the shock that would trickle through my family and friends in the days to come when I had no choice but to combine "I was pregnant" with "my baby died" in the same announcement.

This may seem like a small detail in the big picture of pregnancy and infant loss, but it speaks to the lack of acknowledgment and support our culture is set up to provide moms with pregnancies that end in unexpected loss. Because 80 percent of miscarriages occur in the first trimester,[1] the thought process is that announcing after the first trimester is a sure bet.

The problem? When the majority of miscarriages occur *before* that second trimester announcement can be made, women are left in an isolating conundrum: How do I reach out to people I need support from for my loss when they don't even know I was pregnant in the first place? It's yet another added layer of complexity in the grief of processing pregnancy and infant loss.

Tears of Joy, Tears of Shock

The day after the big surprise dinner that sent my mom (and all of us) into tears of joy and elation, my mom and I spent the majority of the day hauling beautiful magenta hydrangeas from Home Depot out of the trunk and into what would become our first home's garden. We shoveled and dug into the dirt, the spring sun warm on our backs as we carefully tended to this new garden of life being planted outside our yellow house.

Midafternoon, I noticed some stomach pains. Maybe I was just hungry? Mom and I had run six miles at the beach that morning, one of our favorite things to do together. Maybe I had pulled a muscle? And then I wondered whether my pregnant body could handle the same amount of physical activity I was used to. Had I overdone it? *I'll give it some time*, I thought. I drank some water, then back to the garden I went.

It's not lost on me that I was working in a garden when the physical signs of my miscarriage began. It was as though I was being prepared to enter the garden of Gethsemane with Jesus just a few short hours later, the place where I'd meet him face-to-face, drenched in tears and soaked in shock, and ask for my cup of suffering to be taken away.

From the Highest High to the Lowest Low

With pregnancy and infant loss, *everything* changes so quickly. For some women, only days separate the excitement of the positive pregnancy test and the first drops of blood. Sometimes it's weeks, and for some, it's the entire length of the pregnancy.

All losses are traumatic and painful, but the loss of a pregnancy involves a rapid fall from a peak of human emotion to an absolute low of human emotion that is unlike most other forms of loss. When you're newly pregnant, you hold a heightened level of expectation and excitement for your future. New dreams, new hopes, and the adventures of motherhood are on your horizon. Hopes are high. Anticipation is real. And often without warning, when the signs of loss begin, you're kicked off the mountaintop and forced to descend to the bottom of the valley at rapid speed. You go from the highest high to the lowest low in a matter of seconds.

One mom put it this way: "In the case of a miscarriage, it doesn't matter how far along you were. Having the pregnancy experience and the growing life inside that you were so excited about ripped from your grasp is the most painful thing in the world."

Elevated Emotional Descent in Pregnancy Loss

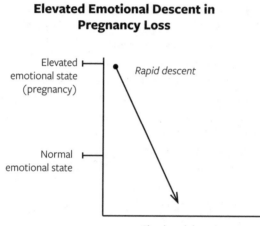

I'm never an advocate for comparing one form of loss to another, but this example may help put into perspective the rapid descent of the emotional experience of pregnancy and infant loss.

My aunt was fifty-one when she died unexpectedly. Three weeks prior, she discovered advanced stage breast cancer that had spread throughout her body and was devastatingly too late to treat. Even though our family was hopeful some medical intervention might be able to keep her alive, we very much felt the shock of this unexpected turn from my aunt's seemingly healthy life. We had three short weeks to process the possibility of her life ending too soon.

Before my aunt's cancer was discovered, I would have rated my emotional state and feelings toward her as loving and healthy. They were not feelings of high expectation or active anticipation; we had simply been enjoying the normal status quo of our aunt-niece relationship. When my aunt died, my emotions plummeted to that valley floor where I felt the deep shock, grief, anguish, and pain of loss. But in contrast to pregnancy and infant loss, the fall of my emotions was not as dramatic (although sharing years of life and memories with someone adds layers to grief we do not experience in pregnancy and infant loss) because my starting point was at a normal level of human emotion and not on a peak. I had, after all, "been *expecting*."

Normal Emotional Descent in Traditional Loss

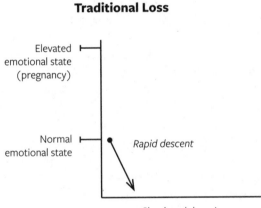

The Shock of the Supper

I imagine Jesus's disciples experienced a mountaintop-to-valley descent of their own as Holy Week progressed. Palm Sunday confirmed their long-awaited Messiah was finally here. The announcement of this would've sent shockwaves of anticipation and excitement through their bones—they had hoped, waited, and prayed for this moment for decades. Was Jesus-on-a-donkey the type of Messiah anyone had expected? Certainly not. But the disciples had been witnessing Jesus upset the religious system time after time for three years. He was not who they thought he was, but they were deeply hopeful that this was the moment that would change everything.

And then Jesus told his disciples, "As you know, the Passover is two days away—and the Son of Man will be handed over to be crucified" (Matt. 26:2).

This was not the first time Jesus told his twelve closest friends this shocking news. It was the fourth and final time in the Gospel of Matthew that he would warn the disciples of his looming death, yet I'm not sure they were able to make sense of it all. How could they? Their only understanding of a Messiah was the equivalent of a superman figure today—one who would be ultimately triumphant, not one who would be subjected to a humiliating, mortal death.

And if you're curious why Jesus connected his pending crucifixion to Passover, there's a backdrop of significance happening we don't want to miss. It was customary for Passover Festival to begin with killing a lamb, and this Passover, Jesus—known as the Lamb of God—would be the one sacrificed. Passover Festival was the celebration of God's people being freed from their slavery to Egypt as God's angels "passed over" the Israelite homes that had been marked with the blood of a lamb, sparing them from death. In the same way, those marked with the new blood of the Lamb (Jesus) are spared from the finality of death today.

What happens during Holy Week has radical implications for life as we experience it today.

But the emotional ride for the disciples was not spared of pain. Just days earlier, on Palm Sunday, they joined with the crowd's shouts: *"He's the Messiah! He's really here! It's really happening!"* A peak of anticipation, a dream coming true, a hope fully realized, an emotional high. Then days later, they descended from expectation to shock as Jesus told them he would soon be gone. Does this sound familiar?

We went to our twenty-week ultrasound feeling what I imagine many first-time parents feel: nervous but incredibly excited to see

42

our beautiful babe. When my midwife sat us down to tell us something wasn't right with our son Morgan . . . we were completely shocked.

Melissa

I'd woken up that morning pregnant, and now I wasn't.

Carrie

I was curious to better understand the shock other loss moms felt when the onset of their loss began. I asked four hundred moms this question: *When you first realized miscarriage/loss was potentially occurring in your pregnancy, what degree of shock did you experience?* Twenty-seven percent said they experienced "moderate shock—I knew miscarriage/loss was a possibility," but an overwhelming majority, 72 percent of surveyed loss moms, said they experienced "absolute shock—I was in disbelief." If you were stung by shock in your loss, you share this experience with the vast majority of loss moms.

In the shock of the first signs of loss, the mind goes into self-protection mode, almost dissociating from the current reality, hanging in a state of disbelief.

That Memorial Day weekend, I knew my unexpected bleeding was not good. I knew what it was pointing to, but my heart and my head refused to connect. My hopeful heart could simply not accept that my baby was dying.

"When evening came, Jesus was reclining at the table with the Twelve. And while they were eating, he said, 'Truly I tell you, one of you will betray me.' They were very sad" (Matt. 26:20–22). In the thick of their shock and sadness, Jesus restated what their hearts and heads could not connect as reality: "The Son of Man will go just as it is written about him" (v. 24).

Do you remember this moment in your miscarriage or stillbirth? The moment when your head gently whispered to your heart: *I'm so sorry . . . but this is actually happening.* It was in this moment of my own miscarriage that I felt God was as far away as the planets in space. How could he allow this? How could the excitement of a dream turn into the shock of death in a day's time? *Surely God isn't in this*, I told myself. *Surely he doesn't understand.*

As the years after my miscarriage went by, I slowly began to see that Jesus *did* in fact understand. He had journeyed hand in hand with his closest friends as they went from the mountaintop to the valley, from expectation to death, from highest hopes to crushed dreams. He was in it each step of the way.

From Shock to Anguish

My bleeding was only getting heavier. Hour by hour, it felt as though God was not only far from me but that he had also turned his ear away from my desperate pleas. Things were getting worse, not better. I gave my husband, Mark, that look that said what we were both thinking—it's time to go to the hospital. Translation: It's time to acknowledge this unthinkable situation *could* become our reality.

I got checked into the ER and proceeded to wait in the overcrowded, funky-smelling waiting room full of the kinds of characters you can imagine would inhabit an ER late on a Saturday night. The woman next to me was grieving a severe migraine, and the man across from me voiced his grievances about a hurting foot every time the nurse walked by. I sat there, silently holding what felt like the heaviest secret and pain to bear, the possibility that the child inside me was dead.

Following a few inconclusive ultrasounds and a cold visit from the young, on-rotation ER doctor, I was sent outside to wait for the results of the bloodwork testing my hCG levels. I found a small, unoccupied concrete bench a few feet removed from the outside entrance. My mom set a bag with dinner from Chick-fil-A on the bench with me. In the swirl of the day's shock, I lost track of when I had eaten last.

This bench became my real-life garden of Gethsemane—the place where I retreated from the noise and allowed my shock to turn to anguish. This is where I pleaded with God to take it all away, to come in with some grand sweeping gesture and save the day at the last minute by turning this whole nightmare around.

Do you remember the place where your shock turned to anguish, where your desperation yielded passionate cries for God's intervention?

I'll never forget that bench.

Entering the Garden

The garden of Gethsemane scene in the Bible had been familiar to me before my loss; it was what we'd read at church on Good Friday to remember Jesus's suffering before his crucifixion. But on that Memorial Day weekend in 2017, the story was no longer just a distant scene to imagine. I was personally invited into it. I entered my own garden of pain and suffering, and though I certainly didn't feel it at the time, Jesus was already in the garden. He was more familiar with pain than I knew as I sat on that bench, living out a similar anguish.

After the shock of the Last Supper, Jesus retreated. We see him process his very human emotions while staring death in the face:

> Then Jesus went with his disciples to a place called Gethsemane, and he said to them, "Sit here while I go over there and pray." He took Peter and the two sons of Zebedee along with him, and he began to be sorrowful and troubled. Then he said to them, "My soul is overwhelmed with sorrow to the point of death. Stay here and keep watch with me."
> Going a little farther, he fell with his face to the ground and prayed, "My Father, if it is possible, may this cup be taken from me. Yet not as I will, but as you will." (Matt. 26:36–39)

Luke's account of this moment in the garden of Gethsemane provides further detail: "And being in anguish, he prayed more earnestly, and his sweat was like drops of blood falling to the ground" (22:44).

The weekend of my miscarriage, I saw drops of my own blood and much more. I saw my heart become crushed outside of my body, my hope deflated like a balloon meeting a rudely invasive sharp pin. I was faced with accepting an invitation to a place I never wished to be. In my own garden of grief on that hospital bench, I, like Jesus, pleaded and pleaded with God to take this all away as I melted into anguish.

Anguish is a particular stage in the grief journey. Researcher Brené Brown defines anguish as "an almost unbearable and traumatic swirl of shock, incredulity, grief, and powerlessness."[2] Anguish is what you felt when the jolt of pregnancy and infant loss became a possibility for your pregnancy, mixed with disbelief, sadness, and complete helplessness. Brown nearly perfectly articulates the experience of Jesus melting in anguish before God in the garden as her definition expands: "Anguish often causes us to physically crumble in on ourselves, literally bringing us to our knees or forcing us all the way to the ground. . . . The element of powerlessness is what makes anguish traumatic."[3]

I hear the echoes of this powerlessness in loss moms' stories regularly.

> I went in for a routine appointment at thirty-seven weeks and discovered there was no heartbeat for our baby girl. I remember begging and pleading with the doctors and ultrasound technicians to keep searching for the heartbeat. I couldn't comprehend what was happening to me and my baby. Those moments felt like a blur, yet they remain vivid in my memory.
>
> Sonia

When faced with your worst nightmare—your baby dying from within you—you enter a place of anguish like this. There is no other place like it. None of us want to be in this garden of grief, just as I suppose Jesus felt in his own garden over two thousand years ago. If this is a place that even Jesus pleaded to be spared from, it should be no surprise that you and I would have a similar reaction. Yet, still, pregnancy and infant loss invite us here.

And what can be found once we arrive? When you enter your own garden of grief, the moment when your shock turns to anguish as you realize your baby is actually dying, you find Jesus there. Not holding a magic wand in his hand. Not pointing his finger at you as though you deserved this.

Where can he be found?

On his knees too, buckled under the weight of anguish. Waiting for you. Suffering with you. Sharing in your pain. Crying beside you. Entering your world of soul-crushing grief without missing a beat, because he's been there before.

Quite a bit of time had to pass before I realized Jesus was in this garden of grief with me, that he cared enough to enter my world of shock and anguish.

I'm not sure where you are today. Maybe you felt Jesus's peace and presence the first moment you knew something was awry with your pregnancy. Perhaps your head knows that Jesus understands pain and suffering, but you don't feel him walking this painful road with your hand held tightly in his grip. Or, like I felt, maybe you're convinced God is nowhere in your pain and your pleas for rescue are continually falling on closed ears.

Wherever you find yourself spiritually when you enter the garden of grief, it's important to know you won't stay there, and neither did Jesus. Holy Week continues on. The garden is a sacred space where life and death intersect. The leaves of old are buried deep in the soil, painfully giving way to death, where eventually new life of the resurrection will grow.

Although it can feel impossible to fathom now, just as I assume Jesus struggled to wrap his head around resurrection stemming from his present garden pain, I remind you of this truth simply to plant hope on your horizon. You do not need to believe in or even desire life beyond the garden yet. But, friend, be reassured that the anguish, shock, and pain of your garden of grief is seen and felt by the creator of the universe.

As you turn and face God in the journey ahead, along with your questions, doubts, and unmet expectations, I pray you'll be surprised by an unlikely encounter with this suffering Savior who not only knows the pain you carry firsthand but also cares enough to walk with you through each step of the grief of your baby dying.

Jesus's story didn't end in the garden, and neither will yours. In time, you'll walk out of this garden—together.

four

Friends Who Fell Asleep

Jesus remains alone with his repeated cry, his fear of death, his insane hope.

Dorothee Soelle

The garden of grief is a complicated place to be. This type of garden is weeded with isolation. As we'll see later, most of our families, cultures, and churches lack a strong framework for coming alongside us in the midst of pregnancy or infant loss. The garden of grief can also feel incredibly lonely because, just like Jesus, we may feel abandoned by God. In the garden, we're vulnerable before God and desperately pleading for a miraculous intervention, while simultaneously wondering if he's even listening. As time in this fragile garden space progresses, it becomes clearer and clearer that the cup of suffering we asked God to take away is here to stay. Jesus knows what this agonizing disappointment feels like, and he knows how that cup of suffering tastes. Like Jesus, most of us in the garden ask for two things—help from God and help from those closest to us.

Just when it looked like it couldn't get worse for Jesus, look what happened after he made his first plea for God to remove the cup of suffering.

Then he returned to his disciples and found them sleeping. "Couldn't you men keep watch with me for one hour?" he asked Peter. "Watch and pray so that you will not fall into temptation. The spirit is willing, but the flesh is weak."

He went away a second time and prayed, "My Father, if it is not possible for this cup to be taken away unless I drink it, may your will be done."

When he came back, he again found them sleeping, because their eyes were heavy. So he left them and went away once more and prayed the third time, saying the same thing.

Then he returned to the disciples and said to them, "Are you still sleeping and resting? Look, the hour has come, and the Son of Man is delivered into the hands of sinners." (Matt. 26:40–45)

In the final minutes in the garden of Gethsemane, Jesus was *betrayed*.

Betrayal sounds extreme, but it simply means "to fail or desert especially in time of need."[1] Did you catch what happened multiple times in our story? Jesus asked his disciples to keep watch and cover his back while he poured out his soul before God. And what happened? They fell asleep. Jesus asked those closest to him to do something he really, *really* needed in his darkest hour. Jesus counted on them, and they failed him. Jesus was suffering, and he was deserted.

Friend, if you turned to those closest to you when your baby died and they failed to come alongside you, you are not alone. If you felt that sting of betrayal from thinking you could count on someone in your darkest hour and they walked away, you share that experience with Jesus Christ.

The Disappointment of Betrayal

Simply put, Jesus's disciples did not understand their assignment. They were unable to wrap their minds around the weight of the needs Jesus had when he was in a state of anguish. They probably had no grasp of the desperation Jesus was carrying. This was not just another bump in the road of life; this was a time when Jesus needed his support circle to come through and have his back. It's important to note that the disciples didn't physically leave Jesus in this critical moment. They were there, in the background, but their silence stung. They fell asleep at the wheel. And sometimes, that can feel worse.

As loss moms, we share this garden experience with Jesus. We assumed we could count on those closest to us to intervene and show up with support when we needed them most. We also assumed our bodies would carry a healthy pregnancy to term and deliver a living baby. But for many of us, in our darkest hours of loss becoming reality, it felt a lot like our bodies—and our support systems—fell asleep at the wheel.

Of the loss moms I surveyed, 35 percent said their loss had a negative impact on their relationships with family/friends, and 70 percent said their loss negatively impacted their relationship with their body.

When I asked loss moms what level of support they feel today, 42 percent said they felt initially supported after their baby died but wish family/friends would do more to remember their baby as time passes; 23 percent said their baby is rarely or never spoken about among family/friends; and 34 percent said they felt family/friends do their best to intentionally remember and honor their baby.

I hear it all too frequently from friends or family members of a mom who has experienced loss, including friends who made confessions to me after my own miscarriage—"I didn't know what to say to you, so I didn't say anything." I have understanding for that—not everyone has experienced a miscarriage or stillbirth. But at the same time, I want to gently encourage you to not let worry over saying the wrong thing keep you silent. The loss mom in your life *desperately* needs your love and support, even if you feel unequipped for the assignment.

The Role of Empathy

Jesus began to feel betrayal as death lingered on the path before him. It was looming. Time was ticking. So it is with loss moms. We begin needing support of loved ones as soon as the bleeding or cramps or "no heartbeat" ultrasound appointment occurs, not just once our baby is gone. So, what's the best thing you can receive if you're a loss mom (or give if you're supporting a loss mom)?

Empathy.

Empathy does not mean knowing all the right things to say or do. Empathy doesn't require you to lose a baby to respond and support the woman in your life who is losing her baby. Empathy goes beyond sending flowers or a one-time text (although those can help). Empathy is a posture of openness to walk alongside another in their time of need.

When I was knee-deep in the shock of my miscarriage, I couldn't wrap my head around people feeling like they "didn't know what to say" to me. I was really hurting and my world was collapsing; their worlds seemed still stable—couldn't they figure out *something* to say? In recent years, I've been humbled to catch myself on the sidelines of other people's losses feeling the exact same hesitation and uncertainty. *What do I say? I haven't been in their shoes. I don't want to say the wrong thing, say too much, not say enough . . . ugh.* In those moments, the Holy Spirit gently reminds me of what I needed most in my own grief: empathy.

Trauma healing specialist Brianna Leiendecker writes that

> a common misperception about empathy—especially in situations of trauma, suffering and grief is that you must have experienced a situation yourself to fully empathize with another person. But empathy does not require sharing the experience . . . nor is it about pretending to have had such an experience. It requires only a willingness to enter into that person's experience and walk alongside them. Empathy is not about us and what we know; it is about the other person.[2]

Empathy is one of the most helpful antidotes that can be offered to a grieving mom. Pregnancy and infant loss are a layered web of complex grief, and not every mom has a fellow loss mom in her corner who has been in her shoes before. But empathy is something that *anyone* can give.

When signs of my miscarriage began, I felt a swirl of confusion, shock, and disbelief. I needed someone to sit with me. I needed a gentle voice to say, "I'm really sorry for what you're experiencing" and "I'm going to be right here for whatever it is you need on your days ahead. I'm not going to leave you in this pain." I didn't need perfect words—they weren't going to take my pain away. I didn't require someone to have lost a baby in order to comfort me in my grief. My heart needed a hug and someone to show me in physical form that I wasn't alone and to help me pick up the pieces of my heart, life, dreams, and hope in the months ahead.

The week I returned to work after my baby died, one coworker knocked on my office door and asked if she could come in for a minute. (This was actually refreshing. It felt like most people wanted to avoid me because they didn't know how to or want to acknowledge my experience). This coworker came in and just said, "Rachel, I'm so sorry. And I love you." She gave me a hug, held me tight in her embrace, and let me cry on her shoulder. It was simple. And for me in that moment it was enough.

A Letter to Our Loved Ones

I wrote an open-ended letter summarizing my own experiences and that of other loss moms regarding the challenging feelings of disappointment and betrayal from close friends in the wake of loss. The amount of response and traffic this letter received was astounding—and sadly, it confirmed the commonality of these feelings.

Dear friend,

My baby died. I'm not the same person I used to be. I wanted to let you know about who I am now. I am a mom, and I am a mom who thinks about her baby all the time, just like moms with living children do. You won't make me suddenly sad if you ask me about my baby. No matter how much time passes, it would mean the world if you asked about my baby. Please say their name. I may cry, and that's okay. My child in heaven is part of my family, and I love when they are acknowledged too.

This might be hard to understand, but I won't "get over" my baby dying. I am also grieving my hopes, my dreams of a family, the loss of who I used to be, and what might have been.

In my grief, there are a few things I keep hearing that hurt more than help—things like "I can't imagine," "You can try again," "At least . . ." and other well-meaning attempts to find a silver lining to my baby dying. I don't expect you to know what to say. My pain can't be fixed, nor would I put that expectation on you. I don't need a fixer; I need a friend.

Can I make one request? Please don't leave me in my loneliest season. I may be a mess, but I still need you. This is all new territory for me. If you don't know what to do, tell me you love me. Give me a hug. Put dinner on my doorstep. Text me that you're thinking of me and my baby. Please don't forget about my baby—or about me.

Love,
a loss mom

If you're reading this book to better understand and support a loss mom in your life, thank you. Thank you for making a selfless sacrifice to step into the experience of another and embodying empathy in this beautiful way. I've created an appendix at the back of this book with a list of loss mom–recommended things to say and do when someone you love has experienced pregnancy or infant loss. I hope that resource will help you feel more equipped to provide love and support when the loss mom in your life desperately needs it.

If you're reading this book as a loss mom, pick some items from the appendix that resonate with you and send them to those asking what they can do for you. It can feel awkward to honestly ask for what you need, but one thing I learned the hard way was that I couldn't expect those around me to know exactly what I needed.

They loved me, but they weren't mind readers. As I became more comfortable asking for what I needed in my grief, I found that when I could clearly communicate what was helpful—what dates I wanted remembered, how they could acknowledge my baby's life, when I needed a meal dropped off, and phrases I did and didn't like hearing—it brought a clarity that erased the tension of unspoken expectations. I realize you may be thinking, *If they really loved me or really cared, I wouldn't need to tell them what I need*, and I understand that. But just like in any healthy relationship, open and clear communication of expectations and needs doesn't thwart the action of love. It helps it.

Their Eyes Were Heavy

Friend, lean in close for this important reminder. The disappointment you may be carrying from the betrayal of your support circle is a *valid* feeling, but that does not mean they don't care about you. In the shock of grief, it's tempting to believe that *everything* is stacked against you and no one, not even your own body, is *for* you. This is simply not true. You are incredibly loved, and when it feels like nobody can understand, be reminded that Jesus has also walked quite a few miles in the shoes of shock, anguish, betrayal, and disappointment.

I don't think the disciples fell asleep—multiple times—and missed the opportunity to meet Jesus's desperate need because they lacked resources or didn't know what to do. Jesus articulated what he needed from them very clearly. And I don't think they failed to step up to the plate when he needed them most because they didn't care. We know they loved Jesus very much—they had left behind their jobs, families, and homes to follow him. So why the missed opportunity? How could they watch the one they loved be crushed to the point of anguish and still fall asleep? Matthew 26:43 sheds insight: "When he came back, he again found them sleeping, because their eyes were heavy."

Jesus's time on earth was coming to an end, but the lives of the disciples were still going. Jesus's needs were desperate, with narrow focus in his anguish, but the disciples' needs were fairly unchanged. Their eyes were heavy. In other words, their worlds did not stop when Jesus felt his soul being crushed to the point of death. Their very human needs were not brushed aside for a need they couldn't fully understand of someone else.

How many of you have felt this exact tension and disappointment in the midst of your baby dying? It feels like your world has stopped and the entirety of your thoughts, time, and emotions has become solely narrowed in on the loss you are experiencing in real time. As your soul is being crushed to the point of anguish, you find yourself in such a deep experience of pain that all lesser things are brushed aside. After all, nothing feels of greater importance than tending to the life and dreams of your child being emptied from within you.

How can they not understand?

If they love me, how can they not comprehend how much this hurts?

How can their worlds keep going?

These were some of the questions that kept my head swirling at night, and this is a tension felt in many forms of loss, not just pregnancy and infant loss. It feels cruelly unfair that the world keeps spinning around you when yours feels like it has abruptly halted. It felt like salt in my fresh wound to return to work after my three paid bereavement days expired. It felt like an out-of-body experience to grocery shop, sit in traffic, walk to the mailbox, and wash loads of tear-stained laundry when my body was still raw from the life that had left it. Everyone else continued on with life, eyes unflinching toward my pain, or so it felt. They had real needs and schedules that did not stop for mine. *Their eyes were heavy* too.

The Descent Ahead

So many factors were beyond my control during my miscarriage—essentially all of them. I was helpless and voiceless but *not* alone. And I wish I realized that sooner. I wasn't alone. I had never been. Despite the isolation of loss, the feelings of betrayal by the doctors and by my body, and the disappointment toward loved ones when I needed them most, Jesus was there the whole time, sitting in my garden of pain, feeling every sting I felt. I was never alone. And neither are you, friend.

So far, we've walked down the mountaintop of expectation on Palm Sunday (*I'm pregnant!*) to the shock of the Last Supper (*It looks like I'm losing my baby. . . . Is this really happening?*) and into the despair of the garden (*Please God, take this nightmare away*). In the next chapter, we'll journey with Jesus out of the garden and toward the final descent of the cross. When death becomes reality, it feels like all hope is finished. But in the silence of grief and waiting that follows, resurrection sits quietly in the wings, ready to make its grand entrance and remind death it will not have the last word in Jesus's story—or your baby's story.

I Get It Now

But before we get there, I want to tell you about a phone call I received one random Tuesday afternoon, three years after my baby died. My younger brother lives in the Midwest, and we don't get to see each other very much, so when the phone flashed his name, I rushed to pick up.

"Hey Craig, what's up?" I asked curiously.

Craig and my sister-in-law Ashlyn were pregnant for the first time, and Craig went on to share that they had just finished their twenty-week anatomy scan.

"Is everything okay?" I'd heard too many stories of loss that started this way.

"Yeah . . . it should be," Craig reassured me. "They found some areas of concern—not everything is developing the way it should be."

Gulp. My heart paused its beating.

"I'm so sorry, Craigy. I know how nerve-racking that type of news can be to receive."

"Yeah, that's actually why I wanted to call you," he said. "I think everything will be fine for our baby. Our doctors will do additional monitoring, and they said oftentimes this sort of issue will resolve itself with time."

A small dose of relief washed over me.

"But there's something I wanted to tell you, Rachel," he continued. "Today I got the first glimpse into our child *not* being okay, and I immediately thought of your miscarriage. You got bad news that didn't have any hope for resolving itself. I didn't understand what you went through a few years ago. But today I saw myself in your shoes for the first time, and I just wanted to tell you—I'm sorry you experienced your baby dying. And I'm really sorry I didn't support you the way I should have. I think I get it now."

Even the seemingly insignificant parts of your loss—like friends and family not showing up in the way you hoped—are ripe for redemption. I didn't expect that God would care enough about these little disappointments to bring healing to them years later. I remember sitting on my sofa after I hung up, healing tears streaming down my cheeks. *God really does care*, I thought. He didn't have to do that for me, but he did.

It was almost like God had been in my shoes and knew what the hurt of betrayal does to a person's heart.

It was almost like I had read the garden of Gethsemane all those years with my eyes closed and now they were opening to see the reality of Jesus's suffering there.

It was almost like my baby dying put me in the garden for the first time, and I was witnessing Jesus dressed in empathy, experiencing the shock, anguish, despair, and soul-crushing grief I was experiencing too. I wasn't alone. I never had been. He had always been there with me in the garden. I closed my tear-soaked eyes on that Tuesday afternoon and muttered, "God, I think I get it now."

five

White Sheets

Near the cross of Jesus stood his mother.

John 19:25

I think the sheets were the hardest part. Those crisp white sheets were a wedding gift, probably the nicest pair we've owned. They had clothed our first bed as husband and wife the past twenty-one months. When I woke up at 5:30 a.m. on May 28th, those sheets were no longer white but covered in the burst of life that was our first child. Seven weeks old. A precious life we had prayed for, dreamed about, and rejoiced over.

I'm grateful I was groggily still half asleep when I stumbled into the bathroom. I had been bleeding and cramping for thirty-plus hours prior, and the ER doctors could do nothing. The pain of my body's inner churnings was now realized. Now gone. I felt life drop from me and flushed the toilet.

When I woke back up later that gloomy Sunday morning, this time fully coherent, there were those sheets—reminding me it hadn't all been just a bad dream. This was my new reality. A most unwelcome, painful one. I walked in and out of our room a couple of times, then started stripping the bed. As I carried the crumpled bundle of loss to the trash bin outside our house, it felt like some really poor attempt to lay to rest this piece of us. There isn't protocol for this stuff.

> Up until now, I've always thought of the loved ones I knew here on earth that have passed and what it will be like to see them with Jesus in heaven. Now we sit in the odd wonder of what it will be like to meet our child one day in heaven—a child we never met, yet somehow deeply knew. A child we will never get the joy of caring for, but trust that God will. We love you, Baby Lohman.
>
> my journal entry, May 30, 2017

It Is Finished

I wonder if time stood still for Jesus between the garden and the cross. It felt that way for me; the clock barely inched forward from the time the bleeding began and when I simply had to wait for my baby to pass from me. Each hour, each bathroom visit, still praying the bleeding would somehow stop and this cup would be taken from me. Then I'd feel like a naive hope-struck fool for thinking any of this nightmare could be reversed. But sometimes you can't keep hope quiet, even in the darkest hours.

In arguably the darkest hour of Jesus's life on earth, he plummeted into despair. He had been disappointed by his support circle, betrayed by one of his disciples, falsely accused by Roman officials, and forced to carry his cross on a humiliating procession to the site of his crucifixion. Beaten, tormented, and insulted, Jesus was hung on a rugged Roman cross next to two criminals. Stripped to his core, it seemed as though the final hope of Jesus's soul escaped in a final plea to his Father.

> From noon until three in the afternoon darkness came over all the land. About three in the afternoon Jesus cried out in a loud voice, "*Eli, Eli, lema sabachthani?*" (which means "My God, my God, why have you forsaken me?"). (Matt. 27:45–47)

The final words of Jesus came from Psalm 22. The tone of the psalm Jesus decided to recite as he looked his death in the face provides further context to his despair, and it became a psalm I read almost daily after my baby died. It more accurately put into words how I felt toward God than any of my thoughts could.

> My God, my God, why have you forsaken me?
>   Why are you so far from saving me,
>   so far from my cries of anguish?
> My God, I cry out by day, but you do not answer,
>   by night, but I find no rest. (Ps. 22:1–2)

If you've felt like you can't tell God how you really feel about your baby dying, Psalm 22 is your permission slip. For the days you carry guilt for feeling like God abandoned you in your loss, the words of Jesus grant you space to freely share that doubt, hurt, and despair with the God of the universe.

Another of Jesus's disciples, a man named John, records further details of the moment Jesus took his last breath.

> Later, knowing that everything had now been finished, and so that Scripture would be fulfilled, Jesus said, "I am thirsty." A jar of wine vinegar was there, so they soaked a sponge in it, put the sponge on a stalk of the hyssop plant, and lifted it to Jesus' lips. When he had received the drink, Jesus said, "It is finished." With that, he bowed his head and gave up his spirit. (John 19:28–30)

Alone

These concluding minutes of Jesus's life on earth are ridden with enough power and sorrow to convince even the greatest skeptic of Jesus's ability to empathize with our pain today. Jesus really does know what it is like to feel utterly alone. And according to the loss moms I surveyed, knowing they were not alone after their babies died was their *greatest* need.

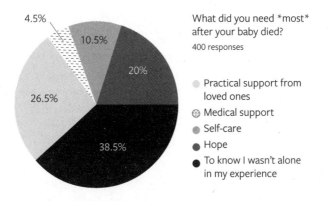

4.5%
10.5%
20%
26.5%
38.5%

What did you need *most* after your baby died?
400 responses

● Practical support from loved ones
● Medical support
● Self-care
● Hope
● To know I wasn't alone in my experience

Friend, I hope you can digest some degree of comfort knowing that while you may feel alone in your experience, the reality is that you are not. Jesus felt betrayed, Jesus felt alone, and Jesus felt grief. The emotions you carry are heavy to process, but Jesus himself can empathize with the load you shoulder.

One of my favorite thought leaders, Tim Keller, summarizes this scene so profoundly. Keller notes that Jesus lived all of his life with God "in a relationship of absolute intimacy and love. But at the end of his life he was cut off from the Father."[1]

I think this part of Jesus's crucifixion often gets overlooked by the parts we can more commonly relate to—physical suffering, false accusations, mockery, and backstabbing by friends. This deep pain of Jesus, which none could understand, has provided me with comfort in my own loss—a deep, internal pain which I've frequently felt nobody really understands.

Keller elaborates: "We cannot fathom . . . what it would be like to lose not just spousal love or parental love that has lasted several years, but the infinite love of the Father that Jesus had from all eternity. Jesus' sufferings would have been eternally unbearable. . . . In the Garden of Gethsemane, even the beginning and foretaste of this experience began to put Jesus into a state of shock."[2]

Does that last sentence apply to your baby dying like it does mine? "Even the beginning and foretaste of [my miscarriage] experience began to put [me] into a state of shock." Jesus has sat with us from the shock of the garden to the pain of the cross, where the core of what he experienced as he hung was abandonment. In his final, well-known cries to the Father, in a moment of honest vulnerability, Jesus echoed the cry of every loss mom as her baby dies: Why has God forsaken me? Why this abandonment? Why do I feel cut off from the one I need most?

Where Is God?

Jesus endured these moments set before him to bear the weight of sin that would have otherwise kept us—you and me today—in a state of complete separation from the Father. Remember the fall in Genesis 3? Jesus's death and resurrection is the unfolding of God's redemption plan. But even more so for us loss moms, we can take to heart the fact that Jesus endured unbearable abandonment so that when you and I endure horrible suffering in life, like the loss of our precious babies, we can find peace in knowing we aren't the first to walk this path. Jesus has gone before us. He can handle you feeling abandoned by God because Jesus, too, has felt that abandonment. He can shoulder your disappointments, your fears, your shock, and your hurt because he has already carried each of these to the cross on his scarred shoulders.

But where is God, who appears silent at the scene of the cross? Why did he turn his head as tragedy unfolded? When my baby dropped from my body around 5:30 a.m., I had a similar reaction. Without conscious thought, I flushed the toilet. Half asleep and without a road map to follow for this sort of tragedy, all I knew to do in that moment that hurt so much was to turn my head. It was all too unbearable to face.

I wonder if God felt that way, too, as he watched his one and only son die. Maybe we can understand his silence; maybe it was all too much to bear. So where is God when death becomes reality? He is nearer than you know. God knows the pain of losing a child too.

God in Our Suffering

It was many months after my baby died before I sensed God's presence in my grief. I knew he understood, but I continued to feel that abandonment Jesus felt on the cross. Where was God *really* in the mess that was now my life? Even though I felt disappointed and abandoned, ironically, I found myself inching closer to God because I was so desperate to find him, to find help, and to find hope.

If you're anything like me, you've been asking yourself, Where *is* God in the midst of my pain and suffering?

The psalmist answers this way: "The LORD is close to the brokenhearted and saves those who are crushed in spirit" (Ps. 34:18).

The *only* way God could really be with us in grief and suffering—and be close to the brokenhearted—is if God himself had experienced the weight of human suffering. It would not be enough for God to have watched from afar. Unlike some of the gods of other religions, God revealed in Jesus is not a stoic, unavailable deity who has distanced himself from the plight of lowly humans. Quite the opposite. In a monumental act of love known as the incarnation, the God of the universe left the comfort of a pain-free heaven to enter our pain-filled world. God with skin on walked this very earth as Jesus Christ. And in the midst of being fully God, Jesus also lived a completely human life, a life nonexempt from the pain and suffering of the world.

As we've already explored in the last few chapters, throughout the Gospels you can also see that Jesus faced the common hurts you and I encounter: the betrayal of close friends, backstabbing, false accusations, the loss of relationships, the pain of loved ones dying, and the crumbling of friends to illness. And then, ultimately, Jesus experienced a pain we haven't experienced firsthand: a humiliating and brutal death on that wooden cross.

God, through Jesus, went before us in all experiences of suffering and pain—those tears he shed, the anguish he sweat, the weight of his soul crushed to the point of death. All of this is not merely a fictional tale of an unrelatable hero prototype. This is the truth of Jesus's life, a path of pain he walked not only to fulfill God's plan but also to offer you, in the midst of your own suffering, a hand that can comfort, a shoulder strong enough to catch tears, and a heart that truly understands what it means to feel the hurt you hold.

It was not enough for God to merely sympathize from afar with the suffering and grief of his people. He entered our world in incarnated human form so that you and I would be able to connect to a God today who really does *empathize* with our sufferings.

Author Jeffry Zurheide adds, "Through Christ, God becomes experientially one with humankind. A bond of ultimate solidarity is achieved through the incarnation. Thus, as Jesus was rejected, God was rejected; as Jesus wept, God wept; as Jesus experienced profound suffering, so also God experienced the same."[3]

How does the incarnation change your grief?

I am continually encouraged by the perspective of author Jerry Sittser amid the grief of losing his wife, mother, and youngest daughter all to a drunk driver striking their car. He writes:

> The Incarnation means that God cares so much that He chose to become human and suffer loss, though He never had to. I have grieved long and hard and intensely. But I have found comfort knowing that the sovereign God, who is in control of everything, is the same God who has experienced the pain I live with every day. . . . No matter how deep the pit into which I descend, I keep finding God there. He is not aloof from my suffering, but draws near to me when I suffer. He is vulnerable to pain, quick to shed tears, and acquainted with grief.[4]

Knowing that Jesus is well-acquainted with grief changed everything about how I processed my own grief. Knowing this truth did not suddenly make my grief lighter or less complicated. But it gave me a way to grieve with hope like the first-century church planter Paul writes about in 1 Thessalonians 4:13. How in the world does a broken person grieve while still holding hope? The answer is found in holding tightly the hand of the suffering servant, the one despised and rejected, the one well-acquainted with grief.

Well-Acquainted with Grief

If someone asked you to describe what you believe Jesus is like, how would you answer?

I often hear people describe Jesus with positive words and phrases, like comforter, someone who did the right thing, morally admirable, kind, generous, and pure. I grew up imagining Jesus as a peace-loving hippie, all good vibes and feelings, no negative associations. This only-positive view of Jesus didn't hold up very well when the pain of my miscarriage entered my story. Western Christianity tends to emphasize the feel-good parts of Jesus, often leaving out the entire spectrum of negative emotions and experiences that deeply characterized the life of Jesus.

After my baby died, I became curious—how would someone from the Bible describe Jesus? I found my answer pretty clearly. The prophet Isaiah described Jesus in a most fascinating way that deeply shaped my grief journey and continues to impact how I understand Jesus today.

"He was despised and rejected—a man of sorrows, acquainted with deepest grief. We turned our backs on him and looked the other way. He was despised, and we did not care" (Isa. 53:3 NLT).

I've never heard anyone described in such terms. Imagine a friend describing someone they want to introduce you to, then choosing words and phrases like Isaiah used. This does not depict the peace-loving-hippie, only-smiles-allowed Messiah I spent my whole upbringing believing was the fullness of Jesus. This depicts someone who knows sorrow, rejection, and suffering like the back of their hand—and this changed everything for me.

Jesus went from a nonempathetic, nonresponsive, cold, distant figure to a kind friend holding an umbrella for me, inching in close to share my pain empathically. How? By knowing the same pain I knew.

Up until this point, my life was characterized largely by hope, redemption, and a mix of trials and joys. Jesus's life was characterized largely by sorrow. My days are mostly marked with grocery runs, coffee dates, and work meetings. His were marked by pain.

It's almost as though Jesus could be known as a professional suf-ferer, a call he answered not out of obligation or enticing salary, but simply out of love for you and me so that when we find our-selves in a valley of death, we know he is in it with us.

When we get acquainted with this part of Jesus, a key to un-locking a much deeper relationship with God becomes available. I found myself no longer praying to a God I had been taught to believe didn't want my hard feelings, questions, anger, and doubts. I no longer felt the need to hide the true emotions of my heart until I had sorted them out into a passable smile I could wear into church. When I discovered Jesus knew grief *really* well, I discovered a freedom to sit with a familiar friend in the middle of miscarriage. I didn't have to please, perform, or perfect anything—I simply, and finally, got to just be with my Creator. And for the first time, my pain felt understood. He got it.

This was the type of Jesus I wanted to share my pain with, be-cause this Jesus was like a friend who understood, like that person in your life who just gets it even before you say a word. Who else in my life was a person of sorrow? Who else was acquainted with deep grief that I could call on a hard day for coffee? As you have probably experienced, too, most people—even those who deeply care about you—have not the slightest idea how to come alongside you in your miscarriage or stillbirth pain. When you are seeking empathy in your grief, it can be found in the person of Jesus. In Jesus, I discovered the best companion to walk me through my season of pain. There is no therapist, no religion, no friend more familiar with the pain you feel right now who simultaneously cares enough to meet you in the midst of it like he does.

Laid to Rest

The night when I carried those sheets off my bed and into the trash bin is forever stamped in my memory. Every step felt like a march of finality. I was acknowledging death had come and had its way with my baby and my dreams of motherhood. It was like the final scene of my miscarriage being played, not in live motion but in slow-mo. I was laying to rest so much more than my baby, as I'm sure you did too.

The night of Jesus's crucifixion, a disciple named Joseph and a Pharisee named Nicodemus laid the body of Jesus to rest: "Taking Jesus' body, the two of them wrapped it, with the spices, in strips of linen. This was in accordance with Jewish burial customs. At the place where Jesus was crucified, there was a garden, and in the garden a new tomb, in which no one had ever been laid. . . . They laid Jesus there" (John 19:40–42).

Like us loss moms, I imagine Joseph and the rest of the disciples from afar laid much more than the body of Jesus to rest that night. Their dreams of a conquering Messiah had been crucified along with Jesus. To them, a true Messiah would never die a humiliating, mortal death on a cross. They had hoped Jesus was the one who would fulfill their great expectations, but the final week of his life had been a rocky descent from one disappointment to the next, until the descent was finished at the crucifixion.

I wonder if they felt like naive, hope-struck fools for believing Jesus was the one. I wonder if they regretted ever following him. I imagine they felt like they had lost so much along with their crucified Jesus—their time, their dreams, their hope. They probably wondered how any of this could be redeemed.

The disciples' hope had worn the name of Jesus, and now hope had died. Hope had been laid to rest. But even two thousand years ago, while wrapped in sheets and darkened by a tomb, hope would refuse to stay quiet.

PART II

The Silence of Saturday

Stages of Hope:
Despair and Grief

six

A Silent Culture

Saturday was silent, surely it was through.
Elevation Worship, "RATTLE!"

My pen didn't touch the pages of my journal very much in the silent months after my miscarriage, but it did record these cries to God one morning.

You will rescue me from this debris, right? You're strong enough, loving enough, capable enough, and I know you see me still. I need to know you're real, Father. That you haven't turned your back on me. I need you. I have no words of my own to pray, other than the words of the psalmist: "Turn to me and be gracious to me, for I am lonely and afflicted. Relieve the troubles of my heart. . . . Guard my life and rescue me; do not let me be put to shame, for I take refuge in you" (Ps. 25:16–17, 20).

The pleas of silence:
God, are you still there?
I need to know.
I'm asking one more time—please rescue me.

The summer was characterized by deep doubts, soul-searching questions, and the silence of the world around me. God seemed completely quiet. My single follow-up visit to my doctor had come and gone. Nobody was texting to check in any longer. Friends and family had already dropped off meals and flowers. Now the food was eaten, and the flowers were dead.

Sometimes silence sucks.

It did for the disciples too.

We know very little of what the day looked like for the disciples after their beloved friend Jesus was crucified. Perhaps that's because the Saturday that followed their horrific Friday was awfully quiet. Still shocked at the devastation of their loss, the disciples, I imagine, carried the early stages of grief like us loss moms do once the traumatic movement of losing a baby has ceased. Confused, shocked, and traumatized at the new reality of life. The noise was over. Nobody prepares you for the silence after loss.

What Is Silent Saturday?

Admittedly, I didn't even know there was a day called Silent Saturday in Holy Week until a few years ago. I had spent most of my life in the church, but all I ever heard about regarding Holy Week was Good Friday and Easter Sunday. And even when Good Friday was talked about, it was always followed up with "But Sunday's coming!" Not only are we unable to sit in the pain of Friday without fast-forwarding to the hope of Sunday, we act as though Saturday never existed. Why? I can think of a few reasons.

First, we don't like silence. Silence shows up in the form of unanswered prayers, seasons of waiting, doubting, dark nights of the soul, or phases of depression, to name a few. These seasons are uncomfortable. They aren't the highlights of someone's year. Others even feel shame when they experience these very normal dips of hope in the human experience. We prize busyness and use productivity as a vice to avoid feeling the discomfort that comes with silence.

Second, it's a lot easier to live in absolutes—black and white. Certainty is comfortable. Living in the gray is hard. Weathering the unknowns of life requires a certain degree of emotional maturity that few possess naturally. We want answers. We demand to know how the story ends. But realistically, most of life is lived in the middle of the story. Most of life is gray. I've experienced far more Silent Saturdays than I have Resurrection Sundays in my life.

And third, waiting is hard. I've yet to meet anyone who likes to wait. Patience really is a virtue, especially in today's Instant Pot culture that no longer has the time to wait for the slow cooker to finish. When we have instant access to answers on our smartphones and same-day shipping with whatever we need on Amazon, it's no wonder that when life forces us to wait without answers, we can start to feel incredibly frustrated. A well-known pastor and author confessed that his greatest challenge in following Jesus for more than thirty years was waiting on God when things were confusing.[1] We'll circle back to the waiting of Silent Saturday in a few chapters.

Saturday's Significance

No matter how advanced and fast the world around us becomes, we will not be able to bypass the Silent Saturdays of life. Silent Saturdays won't last forever, but when you're in the middle of one, it can feel unending. I'll be the first to gently guide your expectations for what lies ahead—the Silent Saturday of pregnancy and infant loss will be a *significant* part of your journey. I wish someone would have told me that Saturdays last longer than anyone wants them to, but what happens during them is not wasted. In fact, what you wrestle with in your Silent Saturday season will largely shape the faith, hope, and resilience you carry from here on out. Author AJ Sherrill says that silence has the power to reconstruct, and I couldn't agree more.[2]

There's a lot of movement in the first part of Holy Week, just as there is in pregnancy. We move from the anticipation of Palm Sunday and the positive pregnancy stick to the warning signs of loss and the Last Supper, then we head from the anguish of the garden to the death of the cross. But most of pregnancy and infant loss grief is stretched across Silent Saturday, and that's why we'll spend this entire section diving into one of the least-discussed periods of loss. Though most of us would rather skip it than sit in it, God has purpose in the Saturday wedged between the Friday and Sunday of your baby loss experience.

Where Is Hope on Saturday?

I remember morning after morning tucking myself farther into the sheets when the annoying sound of my iPhone alarm pierced through my sleep. Without fail, there would be this foggy thirty-second period as I woke up—a brief breath where I felt good things and hope for the day ahead of me. And then my new reality would hit, crashing down from the sky like a weight of bricks. My baby had died. I was still bleeding, and my body was still more pregnant feeling and looking than not. This had become a dreaded routine I could not escape. As I awoke to face the unbearable pain of yet another day, the morning sun seemed like a cruel reminder of my broken dream of bringing a child into the world. I just wanted to hide from the rest of the world. I wanted to press pause on everything.

But the world was not so kind—it kept going. There was a job to show up to, which required getting out of bed and taking a shower. There was food to prep for dinner and groceries to refill and bills to pay. There were public places to go where people smiled and laughed. I learned very quickly how hard it is to function in everyday life with a broken heart and a hopeless soul.

I didn't realize hope had been living like a balloon hidden in my soul all of the years before my baby died. Sure, I had been through hard stuff before, but there was something particularly hope-sucking about miscarriage. Only after did I realize hope had been the fuel for everything in my life. Hope had been fueling the engine of my soul for three decades. Hope had been getting me out of bed each morning. Hope had been allowing me to dream about my future. And now that tank felt empty. *Is this what hopelessness feels like?* I wondered.

Miscarriage had punctured the balloon of hope in my soul, and the leak was fast. I didn't realize just how much I needed hope to do everything from get out of bed to dream about my future—until my baby died. There's nothing worse than feeling hopeless—afraid to think about your future, stuck, fearing your heart may never be whole again. In hindsight, my hope was never fully lost, but it had been miscarried. Buried deep. I didn't know how to find it again. Maybe that's where you're at today.

There's a word I want to share with you that became helpful in clarifying my emotions in the silent stage of my grief: *despair*. Despair is the third stage of hope, following expectation and shock, and despair is what to call those weeks that are blanketed with a general feeling of hopelessness. Brené Brown says that when hopelessness comes from all corners of someone's life and combines with extreme sadness, despair is the result.[3] You can distinguish hopelessness from despair when you feel like your future will be no different from the sorrow of today. When it feels like every day will be the same and every week is clouded with hopelessness and deep sadness, despair wants you to believe that nothing positive is in the forecast of your life. Despair wants you to believe that hope is no longer on the horizon.

Understanding despair matters in your grief for two reasons in particular. First, when you feel despair, it can be helpful to identify this stage as what it is—a stage. You will not stay in despair. You will move through it, just as you have the other stages of your experience thus far. You need to know that these feelings will not last forever. (Please note: If you are feeling deep despair for more than a few weeks, seek professional help. Therapy was immensely helpful in my despairing stage.)

Second, feelings of despair are a common experience for loss moms. If you resonate with those feelings above, you are having a *normal* experience for someone who has experienced loss. Despair has a way of making us feel isolated, like we're the only one feeling *this* way. Sometimes we just need to know we're not the odd one out in the room. Friend, hear me today—others have felt the way you are feeling too. You're not a worst-case scenario. You're doing your best in a very hard season.

The Silence of Culture on Infant Loss

While I was wading through despair and silence after losing my baby, I came to realize that, outside of a fellow loss mom, very few people have any idea what the unique pain of pregnancy and infant loss involves. And because they don't know and therefore can't understand, what often happens? The pain of moms who have miscarried is minimized, shamed, or altogether dismissed.

I was the first one in my family or friend circle to miscarry. I literally knew nobody else who had lost a baby, and this compounded the shame, pain, and isolation of my grief. But here is the lie we can no longer believe: Just because the world doesn't understand the pain of pregnancy and infant loss does not mean it isn't real. By and large, culture is silent on pregnancy and infant loss.

Think about it this way. There are certain social constructs in place for processing grief and loss. There are memorial services and funerals that provide space for official goodbyes, obituaries to memorialize the life accomplishments of the deceased person, and tombstones to plant permanently in the ground to be visited on special holidays for years to come. There are tangible memories to grasp of the person who died—from photos to clothing left behind to personal experiences and memories stored in the soul. These are tools that aid the grieving process.

If I'm honest, I've been jealous of grievers who have those elements to validate their loss. None of the traditional grieving tools were part of my miscarriage experience, and I felt robbed. I carried a toolbox without tools. I had no formal memorial service, and nobody gathered around to publicly mourn with me. No shoulders huddled close to collect my tears. There was no body to hold. A few flower arrangements were delivered and meals offered, for which my husband and I were immensely grateful, but I've always wished for more. There are no photos with my baby, because my baby never experienced life outside of my womb. We shared no fond memories to replay in my mind on days I'm especially missing my baby. Outside of many tear-stained journal entries and a few mementos I bought for myself to remember my baby, I have nothing.

Even two years later, I still lamented this part of losing my baby. In my journal I wrote this reflection:

> Two years ago today, our first baby went to heaven. While I parent a living child now, I find myself more concerned with not forgetting the day our baby died, his life, and what his death continues to teach me. The strange part of miscarriage grief is you have no memories together to replay as you fall asleep, no smiling faces in photos to reminisce, no objects of sentiment to grasp. It's just this invisible memory of a life that was once part of you, but you never met, like a piece of your heart carried off in the wind. So, this is what I have: an iPhone photo I snapped in the swirl of packing up our old yellow house. This one little bathroom where I wept, losing our baby. To any parent wading through the seasons of miscarriage grief, I hope you know that even though we don't have conventional ways to remember and grieve our babies, their lives still matter and are worth remembering. They become forever part of your heart and story, and the world needs to hear your story.

To be a loss mom in a culture that is silent toward your experience makes the grieving process complex. Without these "public" outlets to release pain and mourn, most loss moms are forced to hold their losses closely, and only closely. Under the silence of its breath, society whispers that our pain is less, our loss isn't "real," and to tell the stories of our babies dying is simply too uncomfortable for others to hear. Close to the chest becomes the only safe space we can store our babies' stories. The silence of society has left loss moms with very few alternatives than to grieve internally.

This is problematic for many reasons, but namely one: If the only safe place a loss mom is given to hold her grief is a secret place, and not with others if she chooses, shame easily creeps in. If the world around you isn't vocally welcoming your experience, its silence shouts a painful refrain: *Your story isn't welcome here. Your type of grief isn't welcome here. Your type of loss is too much, too uncomfortable, too tragic, or too immaterial to count.*

This refrain is simply not true. One of my greatest hopes in my work through Hope Again Collective is to change this narrative and provide all loss moms with a healthy, public opportunity to mourn and grieve their babies through sharing their stories, just like everyone else. Why? Because you, too, have suffered the death of a loved one. Don't let the silence of society persuade you otherwise.

Pain without Comparison

I'm convinced that pregnancy and infant loss are unlike any other types of loss. For the reasons we've already identified (and more to come!), pregnancy and infant loss grief are incredibly unique. It's complicated. Our world doesn't know how to come alongside loss moms to validate and grieve a life it never knew. Yet, of course, none of these factors diminish the loss to us. Our type of loss feels just as real as the death of a loved one we knew for years. To be honest, there are days when it seems harder, because so many questions remain. *How could I miss someone so much without even meeting them? What would my baby have looked like? What would it sound like to hear my child laugh, cry, talk, or pitter-patter down the stairs in the morning? What dreams and future awaited my baby? How can this pain be so deep? Why am I so upset over losing someone I never knew outside of the womb?*

Perhaps the depth of the pain mirrors the depth of the love. And yet, there's this surprise of how much the pain hurts—we often don't realize how much we loved our babies until they are gone. The world around us may not know what to do with that concept, but that doesn't matter. What matters is making the space to validate your loss, granting yourself permission to craft your own grieving tools, and gently whispering a reminder to your heart that you're not crazy for feeling disoriented as you grieve a deep, real pain in a culture that largely does not know how to support your journey. We grieve deeply because we have loved deeply.

If you're ready to do something to publicly mourn the loss of your baby, go for it, friend. Plant a tree. Buy a memorial rock. Invite your circle over for a night of prayer and lamenting. Write a letter to your baby. Release a balloon into the sky. Light a candle. Do whatever your heart is craving to validate the life and the loss you now carry. You may not have all the typical grieving tools available to you, but that doesn't invalidate one ounce of your baby's life. Your child deserves to be remembered and mourned in whatever way feels right for you. Create the tools your toolbox needs to help you fully grieve.

Jesus in the Silence

One of the pervading questions that plagued my mind in the Silent Saturday season after my miscarriage was where was God in it all? Where was God on the first Silent Saturday? Why did God allow Jesus's body to lie quietly in the tomb? Why not just resurrect him right after the pain of the cross?

Where is God in the silence?

He's with you.

I actually mean that. Not in a cliché, trite, Christian bumper sticker way, but in a very real way. Let's revisit what happened to the disciples when it appeared God was silent after the loss of their beloved teacher, Jesus.

On Sunday, before anyone knew Jesus had been resurrected, Luke records what happens as two of the disciples walked from Jerusalem to a village called Emmaus. Luke writes, "They were talking with each other about everything that had happened" (24:14). They had experienced so much within just a few days. Their feelings of shock, grief, and hopelessness were still very raw. Luke notes that their faces were downcast (v. 17). Someone approached them and asked what they were discussing. They had no idea it was the resurrected Jesus appearing before them, asking them this question. The two disciples said they were talking about all that happened with Jesus of Nazareth. "He was a prophet," one said, "powerful in word and deed before God and all the people. The chief priests and rulers handed him over to be sentenced to death, and they crucified him; but we had hoped that he was the one who was going to redeem Israel" (vv. 19–21).

Wow.

Their blunt honesty was captured in a few short words: We had *hoped* Jesus was the one. The answer to our prayers. Our long-awaited Messiah. The fulfillment of our hope. Now, we feel like hope-struck fools.

Do you see where Jesus is when the disciples are confessing their broken hopes?

Walking with them.

Do you see where God is when the disciples were certain he was silent?

Walking with them, in the form of the resurrected Jesus.

Do you know where Jesus is when you confess your broken hopes?

Walking with you.

Do you know where God is when you are certain he is silent?

Walking with you.

Keep walking, friend. In the next chapter, we'll look further into the cultural complexities around pregnancy and infant loss and what cathartic ways we as loss moms can grieve, weep, and hope.

seven

Planting Seeds and Tearing Fabric

Be merciful to me, LORD, for I am in distress;
my eyes grow weak with sorrow,
my soul and body with grief.

Psalm 31:9

Seeds of hope are planted in the silence of grief.

Say it under your breath with me this time: *Seeds of hope are
planted in the silence of grief.*

Yes, something is happening under the surface of the seemingly
stagnant silence. Silent Saturday is home to the roots of transformation, and something below the surface is happening in your
soul as you wade through these muddy waters of loss. I know you
don't want to be here; I didn't either. But it's not all for nothing,
friend. Seeds of hope are planted here.

Typically within Silent Saturday, you begin to experience the
intensity of despair giving way to the next stage of hope: grief.
And as you settle into grief, you may notice your emotions are less
intense at times, but you feel more emotions—a widened array
of feelings—and no days are emotionally predictable. Of the loss

moms I surveyed, the majority (71 percent) said grief was the longest stage of their loss experience. I'm not convinced grief even has an "end point"; it seems to ebb and flow with the seasons of life.

I once read that "grief is the normal but bewildering cluster of ordinary human emotions arising in response to a significant loss."[1] Normal but bewildering—absolutely. A cluster of ordinary human emotions—precisely. Everything you feel in grief is a normal, ordinary emotion. What makes grief complicated is the way these ordinary emotions intertwine.

For many of us, grief is the first time conflicting emotions will be regularly juxtaposed together as we go through the ordinary routine of daily life. And life after loss is highly characterized by this tension. In one hand is sorrow; in the other is joy as you begin to experience beautiful things in life again, like laughter, a good dinner, a sunrise, and memory-making with loved ones. Life becomes marked by "and." It is no longer just happy days or sad days. They dance together to an unpredictable rhythm.

I think of one loss mom's story that exemplifies this reality. Emily was given the devastating news at thirteen weeks pregnant that one of her twin daughters had a life-limiting diagnosis. Miraculously, both Bennett and Brynn were born alive. Emily shared with me that God gave her hope during her pregnancy that she would see Bennett live, and amazingly "she lived for seventeen beautiful days." Now, Emily lives embracing the joy of Brynn's life unfolding before her eyes, while also carrying the sorrow of Bennett's life unfolding only in her dreams.

Loss moms become experts at holding conflicting emotions together. Life and death. Joy and sorrow. Hope and grief. Another loss mom, Mara, affirms her experience with this reality: "After losing Sonia, I have worked a lot on the concept of 'holding both'—be it feeling happy for a friend that got to bring her baby home from the NICU and being sad I did not, to feeling both excited yet terrified to try again for another child. The dichotomies we are capable of holding are astounding."

I've struggled to accept my grief. For reasons we'll continue to explore in a bit, grief carries a negative cultural stigma that causes us to resist the encounters all of us will inevitably have with grief in our lifetime. And that was my experience. What journalist Elizabeth Gilbert writes about grief helped me *accept* my grief. She says, "Grief does not obey your plans, or your wishes. Grief will do whatever it wants to you, whenever it wants to. In that regard, Grief has a lot in common with Love."[2]

Humanizing my grief to an expression of love has been freeing. So if it helps you, frame your grief as love. Without love, grief has no epicenter. Do you feel an increased permission to feel your grief if you frame it as an expression of love?

The Choice in Grief

I once had a seminary professor lecture that grief isn't a linear journey but a spiral. All I could think of at the time were two staircases—one standard staircase with predictable steps like you'd find in a two-story home and one wonky, uneven spiral staircase you'd find in an obscure old mansion or something. I didn't really understand what he meant with that comparison beyond those two mental images. In the last five years since my miscarriage, that's been a resounding phrase in my grief: *Remember, Rachel, this is a spiral. This isn't meant to be a linear emotional journey that makes sense. The next step isn't always predictable, and that's okay.*

There are days in grief when you start to feel like yourself again, days when you taste hope. Then there are other days, when the pain you carry is triggered by a random stranger on the sidewalk, and suddenly you're crippled in grief, feeling like you've made no "progress" in your healing. All of these days are perfectly acceptable. And right smack in the middle of grief's wild spiral is the unexpected enlarging of the soul. Grief will change you. But there's a choice in how you permit that change to take shape: grief can harden your soul or grief can enlarge your soul.

On processing the grief of losing his wife, mother, and daughter in a tragic car accident, author Jerry Sittser describes the soul like a balloon, with the potential to enlarge in times of suffering. He notes that grief "will either transform or destroy us, but it will never leave us the same."[3]

How does that sit with your heart? Do you find yourself tensing up at the possibility that grief could yield something positive through enlarging your soul? Are you open to feeling the weight of your grief as it ebbs and flows, or do you find your heart closed off to the waves of emotion?

Again, change through grief is inevitable. But grief does not *transform* your soul unless you give it permission. You probably know someone who has grown grumpy, pessimistic, and closed off as a result of losing someone close to them. Like a hermit, they are a shell of the person they once were and seem to have the zeal zapped out of them. This is the result of grief hardening a heart.

You probably also know someone who is deeply empathetic, thoughtful, and loving. Their soul is beautiful, but not because their life has been pain-free. On the contrary, their soul has grown deep from weathering losses in life and allowing grief to *enlarge* them. They can sit with others in their pain and extend meaningful compassion. This is the type of person you can have meaningful conversations with over coffee or the friend you can reach out to when you're struggling. Grief expert Elisabeth Kübler-Ross says, "The most beautiful people we have known are those who have known defeat, known suffering, known struggle, known loss, and have found their way out of the depths. These persons have an appreciation, a sensitivity, and an understanding of life that fills them with compassion, gentleness, and a deep loving concern. Beautiful people do not just happen."[4]

I don't believe people choose to let grief harden their souls because they *want* their souls to become lifeless. Instead, and often without realizing it, they are deeply influenced by culture's resistance to healthy expressions of grief, as well as two other institutions that have contributed to unhealthy grieving: the family and the church. In order to consciously choose healthy grieving approaches that will enlarge our souls like the beautiful people in our lives, we must first identify the emotionally *unhealthy* ways we are often inclined to grieve.

Family of Origin and Grief

Each of us grew up with "rules" that either implicitly or explicitly let us know which emotions were acceptable to express in our family. As children, we began learning these rules by picking up on the clues our parents provided. When mom had a bad day at work, what happened around the dinner table? Were her feelings openly expressed and did others respond with empathy and comfort? Or were her feelings stuffed, numbed with an extra glass of wine, as a thick tension covered dinner? What about when we suffered a high school breakup or came home from school emotionally struggling? Were we met with open opportunity to share and connect in response, or did we keep those things to ourselves?

For *most* Western families, emotional hurts are stuffed down deep. We learn quickly from what our families model for us. Dad only wants to connect with me about what I'm doing in school, not how I'm doing as a person. Mom never seems to tell Dad what she's honestly feeling. Extended family dinners at the holidays are full of surface-level conversation. We get the picture. We've been absorbing clues about how each of our families handle emotions since we were kids. What have you absorbed?

I remember doing most of my adolescent crying while tucked into my closet, for fear my younger siblings would see me as weak or my parents would be overly concerned about me. It was simply easier to hide my hurt and sadness than enter into processing and sharing when that wasn't openly modeled for me on a regular basis.

When my aunt died suddenly from breast cancer, my family grieved openly from the time she died to her funeral service. There were tears. Relatives embraced. We said what we felt. And then we returned to our respective homes, cities, jobs, and routines. But what about the ongoing grief work that was still needed? Outside of phone calls and Facebook posts on the anniversary of my aunt's death, I saw firsthand that my family, like most families, lacked a thorough framework for healthy long-term grieving.

When my baby died, the reaction was similar. My husband and I received an abundance of phone calls, texts, cards, and flower arrangements in the week following the miscarriage. We were very thankful, but the outpouring was short-lived. Once more, I found my family of origin was not equipped with a healthy long-term grief framework. During the Silent Saturday season of my grief, I desperately needed to know how to grieve. How could I do the deep work of grief when those closest to me weren't emotionally available?

I took some risks in my grief. I'm sure it made people uncomfortable when I publicly posted about the sadness and pain of my miscarriage. Nobody was asking about my grief, but I desperately needed to connect with people during that time. As humans, we are wired for connection, *especially* in life's silences. I turned to my therapist; to frequent, honest posting on social media; to my journal; to prayer; and I took the risk of answering honestly when certain people would ask, "How are you?"

I was the first person in my family to experience pregnancy loss, but I wasn't the first to experience grief. It was no fault of my family's that a weak framework for grief and loss had been passed on to me; this was simply the inherited generational pattern. But without cultural grieving tools applying to my miscarriage, living in a world silent toward pregnancy and infant loss, and with a weak family grief framework, I broke. I needed more. Like someone walking a new path without a road map, I fumbled to find ways to express the grief of my baby dying. All the while, I've been holding hope that my slightly more open grieving would create more space for someone else in my family to express grief honestly and vulnerably in the future too.

Here's a wild thing to ponder: The way you grieve your baby's death has the potential to change the way your family processes grief.

Jerry Sittser asks, "Is God calling you to transform the brokenness of your past into a legacy of blessing to the next generation? Could that be the plot of your story?"[5]

Consider it another seed of transformation planted in the silence of Saturday.

The Church and Grief

I absolutely love the church, and my husband and I have dedicated our lives to pastoring the local church. Yet one of the saddest realities to me is that the Western church, by and large, has missed a key opportunity to come alongside grievers. Expressing grief in the church feels about as taboo as it does in many of our families and social circles.

I remember once planning a Sunday service with our pastoral team on the topic of grief and loss. We were hoping to create a space of response for the congregation to openly express and bring their grief before God. A big challenge became clear when the majority of the worship songs our church used were upbeat, joyful songs. We scoured the worship libraries online and reached out to friends at other churches, asking for suggestions of modern lamenting songs. All of our efforts led to a disappointing, sobering reality. Very few modern worship songs are built for expressing painful emotions. We settled for the closest match we could find, a reflective rendition of "It Is Well with My Soul."

But if I'm honest, after my miscarriage, I simply did not feel like everything was well with my soul. Where was the hymn for me to hum during the death of my unborn child?

I often felt what many other Christians voice in their grief experiences: Feeling sad translates into not trusting "God's plan." If you are angry at God, you must be backsliding in your faith. And if you dare ask God honest questions in your doubt, you are disrespecting his sovereignty. But the Jesus I read about would say none of these things to grievers.

I imagine Jesus would be appalled at those responses, actually. While Jesus stretches out his tear-stained hand to meet grievers, modern Christian culture thrusts its hand into a pocket of comfort rather than entering the transformative space of grief.

How have followers of Jesus built their corporate gatherings—and lifestyles—around following a suffering servant who found himself overwhelmed with sorrow, more than once, and yet manage not to create space for expressing the suffering God's people feel today?

How is it that two-thirds of the psalms are classified as expressions of lament, but we have no modern lamentations to sing today?

I make this point not to criticize the church but to acknowledge the opportunity the family of God has to become a safe place where followers of Jesus can exhale from the weight of soul-crushing grief. Perhaps we've taken too many cues from culture and far too few from our suffering Savior, the one well-acquainted with grief. We have an invitation to become the extension of Christ's empathy in tangible form.

Healthy Grieving

So, let's get practical. How do we, as loss moms and followers of Jesus, find healthy ways to grieve when culture, family, and the church aren't always providing them?

A few years ago, my eyes were opened for the first time to some Old Testament grieving rituals that are actively practiced in the Jewish tradition today. One Sunday at my church, we were introduced to an ancient grieving practice called *kriah* (cree-ah). *Kriah* is a Hebrew word that means "tearing," and it involves a griever tearing a piece of their clothing as an outward expression of their heart being torn from the death of a loved one. The actual tearing is always performed while standing, representing the strength shown amid mourning. The parents of the lost loved one make a tear on the left side of their clothing—over the heart. All other relatives make a tear on the right side of their clothing. Then, the torn pieces of clothing are worn for seven days following the loss (known as the "shiva" period).

Kriah is a cathartic, ancient practice that provides a palpable expression of the grief, anger, and heart-tearing felt during loss.[6] We see *kriah* practiced multiple times in the Old Testament. While mourning the loss of his children, Job tore his robe (Job 1:20), and when Jacob believed his son Joseph was dead, he tore his clothes and mourned for his son for many days (Gen. 37:34).

As a response to the message at my church, anyone in grief was invited to come to the front, choose a small square of fabric from a basket, and tear the corner. I was a bit apprehensive to stand up and participate, but I was surprised at the healing I encountered through *kriah*. This was the first time I had a physical action available to express the pain I had been carrying internally. There was something about the tension of beginning the fabric tear and the release once the fabric gave way to the rip that was cathartic.

And beyond that, I made a public declaration that morning. I stood up in front of people and owned my grief. I had no idea how much I needed to experience the freedom that came from feeling like I was no longer hiding in grief.

I know very few of us have an opportunity to practice *kriah* publicly. I have spent decades in the church and had no idea this grief tool utilized by giants of the faith, like Job and Jacob, even existed. I encourage you to practice *kriah* at home, either alone with God or by inviting those close to you to join you. If you are in leadership at your church, suggest a response time like this after discussing grief.

Cut some small squares of fabric (an old sheet, a T-shirt, etc.). If the fabric is rigid, begin the tear by making a small cut with scissors. Turn on a worship song that resonates with you or pray a simple prayer like: *Dear God, the weight of my grief is too heavy to bear alone. As I tear this fabric, I surrender the weight to you. I release any shame hiding in my heart. I come out of hiding in grief and declare my heart desperately needs your healing touch today. Amen.*

This Is the Time to Weep

No two people will have the same experience with grief. You may benefit from grieving publicly, while another loss mom may find healing in private. You may feel a desire to "create" in your grief and let your emotions come out through music, dance, or art. Perhaps journaling your feelings honestly and chronicling your grief is most helpful to you. (I found journaling to be one of the safest, most honest ways for me to process my grief with God.)

There's no formula for how to best process your grief. The only important thing is that you *do* process it.

Silent Saturday is the time to start this process. To feel the feelings. To ask the questions. To wrestle with God. To reimagine hope. Don't save this part of your healing for a future pregnancy or rainbow baby. It's a myth that living children can erase the pain of miscarried children. I've found that in having my son a year after my first baby died, I experienced healing moments of joy, certainly—but I also now carry a heightened sadness over what I lost in my first pregnancy. Now I *know* what I lost; I see it reflected in my son every day. All that to say, don't buy into culture's lie that having children is the "fix" to your pain. While this is a painful season, it is a precious season. I made the mistake of rushing the healing process with my eyes set only on another child. I believe that if God has children as part of your future, you'll experience healing *in* the process, but like anything in life, when you don't take time to deal with the root of the hurt, it will always resurface, children or not.

This is your time to weep, to quiet your soul, and to be open to the healing work of grief.

Lazarus

I'm so thankful the Bible records Jesus's personal experiences with grief in honest detail. It's almost like God knew we'd need some help with grief years later.

In John's Gospel, we read that one of Jesus's closest friends was *very* sick. This was not like the times when Jesus encountered sick people on the streets; this one was close to his heart. So much so that the sisters of the sick man, Lazarus, sent these words to Jesus: "Lord, the one you love is sick" (John 11:3). When Jesus finally arrived a few days later, Lazarus was already dead.

We'll pick up more interesting details in the chapter ahead, but notice this: When Jesus arrived and saw Mary and many other Jews weeping with her over the death of her brother, how did Jesus respond? Did he quote Jeremiah 29:11 or scold her for not trusting him more? Did he tell Mary that "everything happens for a reason" or say "at least you have made some great memories with him"? No. Jesus didn't respond like a twenty-first century Westerner. It would have been completely valid for Jesus to tell grieving Mary, "Don't worry, I'm going to resurrect him soon"—because that was the truth.

But Jesus didn't skip past the grief. Instead, "he was deeply moved in spirit and troubled," and upon seeing Lazarus in the tomb, "Jesus wept" (John 11:33, 35).

Former pastor Tim Keller captures the moment between Jesus and Mary best: "Instead of pushing against the flow of her heart's sadness, [Jesus] enters it. He stands alongside her in her grief."[7] When it feels like every cultural norm or person around you is pushing *against* the flow of your heart's sadness, take heart. Jesus enters it with you.

And lastly, isn't it interesting how the Jews responded when they saw Jesus weeping? "See how he loved him!" (v. 36). There it is again. Grief and love. Without a moment's pause, the Jews saw Jesus's grief for Lazarus as synonymous with his love for Lazarus.

The Transformation in Grief

As we've seen, grief is a complex soil, ripe with choices for what to do with all that we're carrying. At a time when none of us want to be making choices, let alone thinking about transformation coming out of something so painful as our babies dying, the changing power of grief cannot be denied.

Grief will either harden or enlarge your soul. Grief has the power to shift cultural, familial, and church stigmas. Grief provides ripe garden grounds for seeds of hope to be planted. You may feel powerless in your grief, but the truth is that you have a choice. You get to decide how grief will leave its mark on your life.

> Mourning does not
> simply become dancing.
> It must be planted

in the soil of hope and good counsel,
watered with the tears
of uncurbed grief
and then harvested
by the choice
to move my feet again.

Justin McRoberts[8]

eight

The Three-Letter Question

How long, Lord? Will you forget me forever?
How long will you hide your face from me?
How long must I wrestle with my thoughts
and day after day have sorrow in my heart?
Psalm 13:1–2

It was my first week back to work after my baby died. I received a text from a student at our church who needed to talk as soon as I could. I had gotten to know her, and although I didn't feel like talking to anyone that day, I texted her to come to my office that afternoon. I was completely unprepared for what happened next.

"So, you know the guy I've been dating? Well . . . I got pregnant."

"Oh, wow, this is big news," I said with a gentle smile, still feeling out her state of emotion. "Do you want to share more?"

"I didn't keep the baby," she confessed, tears welling in her eyes. "My mom told me I was too young. She made my abortion appointment, and we went together."

My already broken heart broke further.

She continued, "I wanted to talk to you about how I'm feeling, because I know you just lost your baby too, so you can relate."

With the words of that sentence, everything in me wanted to step out of empathetic pastor mode and correct her semantics. My baby died, yes, but I had been dying to keep it. Inside I was thinking, *Seriously, God? Is this a joke? It's my first week back to work and* this *is what you dump on my lap?*

The student and I continued talking for the next hour. I listened and genuinely hurt from the pain and confusion this young girl was experiencing. She needed the same guidance, comfort, and hope I did. I hugged her, thanked her for sharing honestly with me, and we prayed together before she left my office. And when the door closed behind her, the blatant unfairness of what had transpired overwhelmed me.

This Isn't Fair

One sleepless night in my Silent Saturday season, I remember giving God a long list of reasons why I deserved to keep my baby who died. I had taken inventory of every pregnant person I knew at the time, including that young student from my church, and made a mental list of why my husband and I were "more deserving" of becoming parents. Have you been there too?

After experiencing a stillbirth and a miscarriage two years later, fellow loss mom Jana recalls these feelings:

> We were surrounded by baby announcements. My husband was in law enforcement, engaging with reckless teenagers getting pregnant left and right while they were strung out on drugs. I couldn't reconcile what felt like God withholding this gift of a child from me and stealing whatever brief hope I had in my two pregnancies.

Fairness, especially if you've been raised in middle-class Western society, is misleadingly taught as something that can be earned. If you work hard and are a decent human being, then you deserve good things. It's like an equation, right?

Beginning in childhood, we are recognized for good performance —even participation. There is no shortage of T-ball trophies and honor roll certificates to clutter the elementary years. Our culture is entrenched in merit-based behavior. We are conditioned to believe that good behavior and character equals fair outcomes (i.e., getting what we want in life).

Let me be the first to say that pregnancy and infant loss *are* unfair. They feel unjust. It feels unjust. God loves justice and hates death. We are right to share in these feelings. But I want to peel away at something deeper—the notion of what we believe we *deserve*.

Not What I Deserved

What our culture has come to associate with being *fair* is actually what we think we *deserve* based on our own good choices or behavior. True fairness, however, is impartial and means we're all subjected to the same amount of good and suffering. And within that framework, *Why me?* becomes *Why not me?* Remember what happened in Genesis 3? The evil and suffering we experience today is the by-product of living in a fallen world. And contrary to what we are conditioned to believe, no one is exempt from suffering. Fellow loss mom and author Adriel Booker reminds us that "suffering does not choose the weak or the strong, the faithful or the faithless. It chooses the human."[1] In the Silent Saturday of my grief, I realized it wasn't fairness I was truly after. My good behavior, choices, and merit hadn't equated to what I thought I *deserved*. And that stung.

If you're like me, you'll add up the equation of what you did right and demand to know why you were the one who had to lose your baby. Friend, I totally get that feeling. I sat in it for a long time. It felt nearly impossible to swap my *Why me?* with *Why not me?* (I still don't enjoy reframing my trials this way.) But then I had to ask myself, What version of the good life have I bought into? The one culture had sold me—that if I did good, I'd be spared pain? This one had been implicitly entrenched in me as a by-product of being raised in middle-class America. But this is so vastly different from the good life Jesus died to offer me.

Jesus didn't promise a pain-free life. Jesus promised a life *with* him. And it's not a life of martyrdom either. A life with Jesus isn't fair; it's better. A life with Jesus says, "When the inevitable suffering of life comes, you won't have to face it alone. And I won't just leave you to pick up the broken pieces. I love you so much and I'm powerful enough to do something redemptive with those pieces." No other divine being promises to sit with you when suffering comes. No other religious figure has had their own life marked by pain, suffering, betrayal, and grief. No other god is powerful enough to bring redemption out of broken places.

Even in suffering, I choose life with Jesus. Do you?

Why Did God Allow This?

I can't tell you how many stories from loss moms I've read that allude to reasons why they think God allowed their babies to die. When suffering hits, we try to make sense of why it happened to us. Here are a handful of questions loss moms say they would ask God if they were face-to-face with him:

- o Why would you let this happen to me? Haven't I been through enough?
- o Why? After having so much trouble conceiving, why take our baby away?
- o Why does it feel like others who seem less deserving or chose to abort their babies get pregnant but not me?
- o What did I do wrong in life to deserve this?
- o What lesson are you trying to teach me?

I read a simple yet profound book that put words to the most common responses to suffering and death and put words to how I was imagining God interacting with the suffering of my miscarriage.[2] (Quick note: Each of these responses to suffering has its flaws. God can and often does work in these ways, either due to human sin or the natural consequences of a broken world.) Which of these resonates with how you view God in your loss?

"God is teaching me something."

The teaching response views God as a professor. God often does use life experiences to shape us, but we rarely pause to address the *type* of teacher we view God to be. Is he the cruel, white-haired, grumpy professor who shouts at his students and cares more about disciplining them than he does fostering their true growth and transformation? Or is he more like your favorite grade school teacher who was smart and clever, loving and kind, and though she pushed you to grow and learn, you knew she truly cared about you? I believe that God cares deeply about your lifelong transformation, and his desire for you is to be shaped more and more into the image of his son, Jesus. But I do not believe that God crafts up lesson plans of evil to accomplish this. We read in the Old Testament that God "does not willingly bring affliction or grief to anyone" (Lam. 3:33). Can God use the pains of your life to grow you? Absolutely. Does God care about redeeming your hurts and losses? Without a doubt. But God does not find joy in your suffering or in "teaching you a lesson." He weeps with you.

"God is testing me."

This is the athletic response to suffering, and as its name suggests, it frames God as a coach who sends us onto the field to see how many hits and tackles we can endure, waiting to see if we can "pass" his test and make it through the suffering. The problem with responding to your suffering with this view of God is that "it distances the coach from the athlete. . . . We tend to want to pass tests alone, especially if we've grown up in a culture that is steeped in approval contingent upon performance. We have come to believe that we must individually achieve, make the grade, take the hit."[3] Job is a biblical example of this. He viewed all of his struggles as tests from God. Job cursed God, gritted his teeth, and resolved to endure the testing. He came to see that God was not hell-bent on punishing him, but rather, that God was with him, loved him, and restored all of his losses in the end. If anyone has reminded you that "God won't give you more than you can handle," that notion derives an athletic response to suffering. But people often forget to include the second part of that notion. In reality, God won't give you more than you can handle *with him by your side.* You aren't meant to grit through suffering alone.

"God is disciplining me."

As you read in the responses from fellow moms, many of us view suffering as something we *deserve* or had coming. We see suffering as the result of an unforgivable sin or wrongdoing. Yes, we will reap the consequences of unrepentant sin in our lives, but this view of suffering goes a step further. It is as though God is sitting on a cloud with a scorecard in hand, meticulously tracking every right and wrong in your life. When the wrongs outbalance the rights, bam! Here comes the discipline you deserve. This view undermines Jesus's powerful work on the cross. God has no interest charging you for the debts you owe—Jesus has already paid them off in full.

Wrestling with Why

As the Silent Saturday season of your grief marches on, you might try to figure out why your loss happened. This is common. We are rational beings by nature, and because pregnancy and infant loss are so personal, it makes complete sense that we want to do all we can to figure out why our babies have died and prevent it from ever happening again.

Asking your "why" questions is a healthy part of grief processing. This is part of wrestling through your experience, and you have permission to let these questions rise to the surface of your heart. If you've been raised to believe that questioning things is not permissible in a Christian tradition, you can wean all the permission you need from looking at Job in his suffering.

Author Peter Scazzero says, "Job shouted at God, he prayed wild prayers, he told God exactly what he was feeling. For 35 chapters we read how he struggled with God. He doubted, he wept, he wondered where God is and why all this has happened to him.

He did not avoid the horror of his predicament but confronted it directly."[4] It's more than okay for you to wrestle with your questions, doubts, and anger directly; it is actually a healthy part of grieving.

Grief puts you in the ring of a wrestling match you never asked to join. There's something about having the injustice of your baby dying blindside you that moves you out of the paralysis of status quo and into a place where you wrestle with deep questions of life, meaning, and God. Loss moms tend to focus their "why" questions on three areas: their body, their doctor, and God. We tell ourselves: If anyone is to blame for my baby dying, surely it has to be one of these three. And we stick to that belief even if deep down we know this isn't true. As we explore these three areas of blame, pay close attention to what resonates with your heart. That resonation will be an important key to unlocking the specific areas of healing you can pursue in the future.

Why, Body?

I knew that babies could die, but I couldn't understand how my body was unable to do the thing it was made to do. Why couldn't my body keep my baby alive and healthy? I knew research was out there that pointed to bodies knowing exactly what to do during pregnancy and that typically a miscarriage is a body's response to an unviable pregnancy, but I simply didn't want to accept that. It felt so cold—this was my child's *life*. And even if my body acted how it was supposed to act, I was still angry about it. How could my body divorce me from my baby in such a traumatic, painful way?

For most women, pregnancy or infant loss is their first (or most punctuated) feeling of their body physically betraying them. This is not an area most loss moms have space to safely talk about either, outside of a therapist's office. Feeling like your body has betrayed you compounds the deeply personal experience of loss after your baby dies. It's pretty uncomfortable to walk around in a body you feel has gone against your dreams.

I asked a handful of loss moms to share their experiences with their bodies during their loss, then I compiled this collective letter from their responses.

Dear body,

I'm pausing to be honest. Since my baby died inside of you, I've avoided you and, often, even hated you. What happened?

I look at my hands. These hands held a positive pregnancy test. These hands wiped blood. These hands wiped tears. These hands have clasped desperately together, pleading for hope. I hope these hands hold a living baby someday too.

I look at these feet. These feet have walked through waiting rooms of pregnant women. These feet have walked cold hospital hallways. These feet have walked aisles of baby clothes. These feet have walked me to my baby's grave. I hope these feet walk a child to school one day too.

I realize now that you're not broken, body. You didn't actually fail me. You were home to an angel. I'm sorry for the nights I've blamed you when you were simply trying to help me survive.

You don't look like other moms, and that's okay. Sometimes I'm sad you look postpartum without a baby to show for it.

But, body, we've been through so much together, and you've carried me through it all. You've been a home to life. You've been a home to death. You're still a home to my heart. And today, I thank you.

Sincerely,
a loss mom

Why, Doctor?

My doctor's bedside manner throughout my miscarriage felt like the coarsest salt in the wound of losing my baby. I sat on the cold metal table for my follow-up visit the first time I met her face-to-face. She verified I had passed all my tissue and told me I was "good to go." She hurried out the door before I could ask—"When will my bleeding stop? When can I resume physical activity? When can I try to get pregnant again?"

I got dressed quickly and headed out of the exam room, wanting this emotionless experience to just be over. She bumped into me in the hall as she rushed to her next patient. "Oh, by the way, this isn't your fault, Rachel," she spurted out nonchalantly.

What was I supposed to do with that? I felt so unsettled.

Loss moms have a wide array of experiences with their doctors, but from the stories I've heard, very few have a *neutral* experience. On the day your baby dies, you and your doctor are on severely different wavelengths. It's a workday for them. It's the worst day of life for you. Yet for better or worse, your doctor is part of your baby loss story.

And because of that, forgiveness has a role to play. I spent months feeling negative about my doctor, as if she could've done something to prevent my baby from dying. I knew nothing she could've done would have changed the scenario, but it felt good to have someone to blame.

I was messaging one night with an old acquaintance named Analiesse. She is a practicing doctor of family and obstetrics medicine. When I shared about my miscarriage experience with Analiesse, she graciously and unexpectedly apologized on behalf of the medical community for the bedside manner I had received.

I became curious. I asked Analiesse what it was emotionally like on her end, to care for women with pregnancy losses and complications on a daily basis. What she shared with me has become the single most helpful tool for processing and forgiving my doctor.

I asked Analiesse for permission to share that same piece of perspective with you, and she graciously agreed. As you read her words below, you won't find answers to the "why" questions you have for your doctor. You also won't find a Band-Aid to cover any wounds you may have from your doctor's response to your baby dying. But what you will find is the very rare opportunity to look at a day in the life of an OB, and this perspective may help lift the blame your heart carries toward your medical provider.

A Day in the Life

I'm Analiesse, and this is a true recorded layout of my schedule on the day I was asked to contribute. My first patient in the clinic every morning is at 9:00 a.m. That day, I thought I would be ahead of the game and get my oil changed on my way to work at 8:00 a.m. I am driving to the shop when the front office staff calls me to say, "Your OB patient Laura [name changed here and in future stories to protect privacy] just walked in the door.... She is thirty-two weeks pregnant and is doubled over, sobbing with terrible belly pain. It's not coming and going like contractions, but she really looks like she is in severe pain."

I make a U-turn. "I'll be there in five minutes," I say. I pull my patient into an exam room, assess that her pregnancy is okay but that she may have a medical emergency going on. I walk her across to the ER, but because she is thirty-two weeks pregnant and experiencing abdominal pain, the main ER refuses to see her. They say it's on me to do whatever workup I want. I put her in a labor and delivery room instead and order all the emergency labs, imaging, IV morphine, and essentially act as the combined ER/OB/medical doctor.

While I am going through Laura's chart, I see a notification that a patient I know super well is in the hospital. Phil is a thirty-five-year-old guy, and I provide medical care for his whole family. His wife texted me the day before to say the "sinus infection" I had written antibiotics for was much worse; Phil wasn't wanting to wake up to eat much, and he was intermittently confused. I tell her to take him to the ER immediately for further testing. Sure enough, his further testing shows a massive brain tumor, and he is now in the hospital with a likely terminal diagnosis, awaiting a massive "heroic effort" brain surgery in the next forty-eight hours. Emotionally, I'm crushed.

I'm back to trying to take care of Laura, my OB patient with abdominal pain. I'm supposed to start seeing patients in five minutes in clinic, but there's no way that's happening. I call my receptionist: "Please cancel my first patient and move him to another day. And reschedule my second patient to be over my lunch hour."

I'm about to hang up with my receptionist when she says, "I'm sending a high-priority message your way. Get to it when you can." Okay, noted.

I finish taking care of Laura. I am still deeply troubled about Phil. I drive to my clinic now, an hour late already. I sit down at my desk and see that message my receptionist had referenced: Twenty-two-year-old Diana, who I have been working extremely close with on an almost weekly basis to get off drugs and get her life back together has been in a devastating car accident. She was airlifted from the scene, is in ICU, and has been cited as driving under the influence. Her dad knows I was closest in her care and wants to talk to me asap.

Okay, deep breath. Monday has just started … and I'm drowning in patient needs, grieving for my patients' families and my own emotional weight, and have a typically busy clinic schedule waiting for me. I have about thirty refill requests, five patients who have called with questions for me, and twenty lab and imaging results waiting for my review.

I have fifteen minutes before my next patient (the first one I didn't cancel). I run through my results as fast as I can. Patient A can get a letter telling them everything looks good, my nurse needs to call patient B and let them know their lab is high and needs repeating, patient C … oh, patient C has been having some bleeding in her pregnancy at seven weeks. I haven't met her yet. She's scheduled for a new patient appointment in a week. The ultrasound I ordered for her shows there has been a miscarriage. Okay, that's probably a patient I need to call myself to tell her there has indeed been a miscarriage.

I proceed to see my patients scheduled for the day. I use the twenty minutes left of my lunch to call the hospital to check on Laura, call Phil's wife to convey my heartfelt devastation and see if I can do anything, and call Diana's dad to learn more about the accident.

I then call my miscarriage patient. "Hey, I know we haven't met yet. I'm so sorry to have to tell you this by phone, but it looks like you have had a miscarriage." I go through the motions: talk to her about how she is feeling, explain her options for pain management, remind her "this isn't your fault," send in the script she desires, and recommend she make an appointment in a week for a follow-up.

At this point, my afternoon caseload started ten minutes ago, the hospital is trying to reach me about Laura, one of the patients who had called is angry I haven't gotten back to her yet, and I still haven't used the restroom, eaten, or drank water, and am starting to feel a bit light-headed from the rush of the day. I use the restroom as quickly as I can. *Pee fast. Don't cry. Hold it together. Keep moving,* I tell myself. I chug some water and am quickly on to the next patient.

Sometimes during a physician's busiest days, patient care has to be triaged into "threatening medical situation" and none. And while miscarriages can be emotionally devastating, at times they are processed in the medical community as, "If the patient is physically okay, I'll give them their options and then see them for follow-up."

I am so sorry for the hurt and pain that this can feed and for the abandonment that can be felt.

I care. On behalf of the medical community, we care. And I'm so very sorry it doesn't always feel that way.

Analiesse Carter, MD

Why, God?

Lastly, we address blaming God. If you've asked "Why, God?" a thousand times since your baby died, you're not alone.

You're also not the first to blame God for allowing death. In the last chapter, we looked at how Jesus wept alongside Mary and Martha when their brother, Lazarus, died. But look at what happened before the weeping.

Martha ran out to greet Jesus when he arrived. "If you had been here," she said, "my brother would not have died (John 11:21). Then, a few verses later, when Mary reached Jesus, she "fell at his feet and said, 'Lord, if you had been here, my brother would have not died'" (v. 32). Both sisters blame Jesus for their brother's death. Their blame does not offend Jesus. Their blame does not cause Jesus to walk away. It almost seems as though their blame shows Jesus just how hurt their grieving hearts are. Jesus doesn't reprimand their blame. Jesus proceeds to weep with them.

If God has felt silent to you, keep crying out. It's exactly what Jesus did. Remember when he was abandoned on the cross? God was silent, yet Jesus continued to cry out to him. Christian culture today makes very little room for doubting or questioning God. It's as though we think asking a question or being honest in our disappointment automatically means we don't believe or are leaving the faith. This is simply not true. What good is a relationship where you can't be honest when you're hurt? We view relationships with honest emotional communication as healthy. Yet when it comes to our relationship with God, somehow this is viewed as the opposite.

Again, we look to Jesus. Deep in the disappointment that God had forsaken him, Jesus's cries of doubt and anger do not indicate he had abandoned his relationship with the Father. If anything, this exchange shows us that Jesus chose to use his last dying breath to declare the foundation of his faith.

The Why Matters

You will likely never get a fully satisfactory answer to all of the "why" questions surrounding your baby's death. What you can cling to, most importantly, is the truth that God sees you, loves you, and weeps with you, even in the silence. This wrestling match surrounding your grief will not last forever. You will not always be up late at night, crying out to God for answers and carrying the heavy weight of blame toward your body, your doctor(s), or God. But even in silence, your wrestling is not purposeless. Keep pressing in.

Grief has a way of causing you to retreat into a cocoon, and as you retreat from the world and question all of your previously held certainties, you emerge from that cocoon with new eyes. Life is no longer the same. We are no longer the same. God is no longer the same to us.

Loss has a way of changing everything around you in profound ways. The transformation of grief does not happen in big and flashy ways. Grief's transforming work happens under the surface, in the middle of the silence.

nine

Reflections from My Husband

Mark Lohman

They say that opposites attract. Well, that's not the case for Rachel and me. (Hi, it's Rachel's husband, Mark, writing this chapter.) Rachel and I are similar in so many ways. While we were dating, and even during our engagement, we rarely disagreed. We were just naturally on the same page, it seemed. In fact, we found our premarital counseling so smooth that we wondered if there was something wrong with us. Why *weren't* we having issues? We share a handful of commonalities: we are both high-achieving Threes on the Enneagram, we love high-quality Chemex pour-over coffee, and we live for traveling to new countries together. Rachel enjoys watching Laker and Angel games with me. We even have the same taste for home decor!

But there are two areas where we have not been able to relate in our relationship: marathons and miscarriage. You're probably wondering, *Marathons and miscarriage? Huh? How can you even include those in the same sentence?* Hang with me.

Marathons and Miscarriage

First, let's address the far more superficial one: marathons. Rachel comes from a running family. Both of her parents run marathons (they've even completed the Boston marathon!). Rachel has been running long-distance since she was a kid and as of now, has run eight full marathons and a dozen or so half marathons. Me on the other hand—I hate running! Not only have I never run a marathon, I simply cannot understand why anyone *would*. Voluntarily training to take your body through 26.2 long, belaboring miles? I don't get it. I literally can't wrap my brain around why anyone does this. I've rooted on the sidelines while Rachel has completed a few marathons since we've been married, and I've heard her recount, both before and afterward, the mental, emotional, and physical battle she goes through to finish a marathon.

And I'll be honest, I just don't understand the experience. Why? Because I've never done it myself. I can't put myself in her shoes. It's hard for me to grasp what it takes to run a marathon—how it makes you feel, the effects on your body, the highs and lows, the mental conflict, the physical preparation. And while I've stood on the side of the marathon courses, cheering her on, on marathon days Rachel and I have almost *opposite* experiences. She's in the thick of it, with mental, emotional, and physical effects to show for it, and I am a bystander.

Let me be blunt. Though obviously in a far more serious sentiment, this is how I've also felt about our miscarriage.

It's been a difficult experience for Rachel and me to find shared ground in our loss. I understand our miscarriage cognitively, but I didn't share her physical experience. My body didn't bear the weight of such loss, and because we experienced the same event in such different ways, our resulting emotions and feelings have also been different. I don't feel like she feels/has felt. As much as I have stood and continue to stand by her side, watching, loving, and supporting her, I'll never fully understand what our miscarriage was like in *her* shoes. We are two very similar people living through one event with two very different experiences.

Men, Women, and Grieving

I'm assuming that the vast majority of people reading this book are women who have suffered loss. My goal in this chapter is to provide a personal, honest window into the mindset of a husband who has miscarriage in his story. Having gone through pregnancy loss with Rachel, having been part of my sister's story of infertility and infant loss, and having pastorally counseled many others over the years, I believe one of the most challenging issues regarding pregnancy and infant loss is handling how both males and females process these types of loss differently.

Let me put it simply. It's been my experience that most fathers do not connect to the emotional toll of pregnancy and infant loss in the same ways or to the same degrees that mothers do. It's not that I didn't care about our baby dying. My heart desperately broke for Rachel and our child. It's that I processed our loss differently and wasn't going through the same thing as Rachel was physically.

Back to the Enneagram that I mentioned earlier. One of the best and most helpful parts of the Enneagram is reading the description of your type. You know you've found your type because when you read the description, you immediately feel like, "Oh my gosh, that's *me*. That's how I think. That's what I'm scared of. I make plans like those plans. I desire that."

When someone puts words to what you're feeling, there's a profound moment of understanding and empathy. One of the brilliant aspects of the Enneagram is that it allows you to understand and learn how to interact with each and every type. All types are different, but we can seek to understand how others think and how we can best work together.

Let me put together a description of how men commonly respond to miscarriage or stillbirth. Of course, this is a generalization and there will always be exceptions. However, for me personally, as well as other men I know, these have been among the most frequent responses and feelings surrounding pregnancy and infant loss from our perspective.

o We are genuinely sad and heartbroken over our baby dying but don't know how to communicate those feelings all that well.

o It's hard for us to relate to any physical pain our female partner is experiencing, which creates a loss of mutual experience and relatability.

o We *may* have an easier time believing the current situation will pass and that there remains hope for having children in the future.

o We *may* be confused why our female partner is grieving much deeper and longer over the loss.

o It can often feel like our attempts to console or comfort with words don't provide enough consolation to our female partners in the moment.

o We grieve the experience we've witnessed our female partner endure in addition to grieving the loss of our child.

Again, this list isn't exhaustive, nor does it claim to cover the feelings and thoughts of every father who has pregnancy or infant loss as part of his story. This was my journey, and I've found it to be the same as others as well.

Also, I should note that I'm being blunt here. I was certainly grieving over this horrific situation. I was heartbroken. I was confused. I didn't know what to do. All of this led to a deepening cavern between Rachel and me, because we were processing the miscarriage differently. Put otherwise, we became more isolated and alone in our grief, despite sharing a marriage and sharing the same loss.

Waiting and Wilderness

Feeling alone, isolated, misunderstood, and confused is what many spiritual writers have described as metaphorically being in the desert wilderness. And within the desert wilderness, we encounter silence. We are disoriented. We don't have answers. We ask ourselves, *Why did my baby die? When will I be able to try again? Will I ever become a parent?* And we're left confused as to why we're experiencing this desert wilderness in the first place. One of the hardest parts of the desert wilderness is that we're often stuck waiting in it.

And our culture doesn't like to wait. I certainly don't like to wait. This is why we want to go straight from Good Friday to Easter Sunday. We aren't comfortable with the silence of Saturday. We don't know what to do in the silence of Saturday. We aren't used to the silence of Saturday. We live with a sense of immediacy because everything in this digital age is at our fingertips right away. Fast food is delivered directly to your house via Grubhub. You can make same-day electronic bank deposits on your smartphone. There's immediate real-time news available on your Twitter feed. I mean, I now think Amazon Prime's two-day shipping is *too slow.* And for all of us really impatient people, this is showcased when we're getting ready to check out at the grocery store and we start examining all the lines to pick the one that will be the quickest. (If we have another person with us, we suggest splitting up so we have two chances of picking the fastest line.) *We don't like to wait.* We don't like not having answers. We don't like living in seemingly silent, isolated deserts. We want to be on the mountaintop, where life is good, struggles are few, distractions are abundant, and loss isn't in our face.

But here's the thing. In a lot of ways, the Scriptures put forward a story of waiting for hope in an isolated, silent, desert wilderness time after time. And as you've already explored, though we live in and settle for the Instant Pot culture, God often works like a Crock-Pot. A desire to fast-forward through the silence of Saturday, to skip the desert wilderness in life, simultaneously becomes a desire for a quick fix. God is after a deeper, high-quality, long-term hope that's best transformed in the desert wilderness.

The great Old Testament prophet Moses spent some forty years wandering in the desert, taking on the seemingly insignificant role of shepherding *before* God spoke to him in the burning bush. Then the nation of Israel, God's very own people, wandered in the wilderness for forty years *before* they entered into God's promised land. Forty years! What could have been an eleven-day journey instead was a long, lonely, dark forty-year journey. King David, a man after God's own heart, wandered in the desert in caves, fleeing for his life for nearly twenty years *before* he was able to rightfully take his throne in Israel as king. In fact, many of the psalms were written by David when he was in a lonely, dark desert. Then you have Elijah, who wandered around in the wilderness for forty days, depressed, suicidal, and hopeless before he encountered the voice of God.

Let's go back to the nation of Israel, God's chosen people. After spending forty years wandering the desert, they finally got in to the promised land. But then they ended up getting captured by their enemy Babylon and exiled into another wilderness experience outside of their home.

And this is actually how the Old Testament ends. With story upon story of God's people wandering alone in the desert, stumbling through days of silence and waiting.

After four hundred years of waiting and silence—without even a peep from God—a strange prophet named John the Baptist showed up. Guess where? In the wilderness. He was, after all, called the "voice of one calling in the wilderness" (Matt. 3:3). And then Jesus himself, the author and perfector of our faith, spent forty days in the desert, being tempted by Satan, before he officially began his ministry.

Every single one of these biblical characters did amazing things for God. But every single one of them encountered the silence of a long desert experience. And it's precisely in that desert experience that their hope was birthed.

As you probably feel, too, the desert season after loss is really tough. It feels dry, silent, and often like the opposite of hope being born again. One of the most surprising parts of our miscarriage was the struggles we wrestled through in the desert that followed. Rachel especially struggled with doubt over her dreams of motherhood and our ability to have healthy, living children in the future. Somehow, I had an odd sense of hope that though our family dreams had started differently than we wanted or ever envisioned, we'd be okay. We didn't need to toss out our dream in the desert.

Grace in the Waiting

Watching your spouse question everything—their body, God, God's goodness, their future, you name it—is another painful experience in the aftermath of pregnancy and infant loss.

So, what did I do alongside Rachel in the waiting?

First, I think it's helpful to be able to name the isolated season for what it is—a desert wilderness (as mentioned above). In some strange way that I can't fully articulate, authentically naming our season reminded us that it was just that—a season. The lonely desert season doesn't last forever. It does not have the last word. No matter how dark and cold it is, winter will give birth to spring. I reminded Rachel of this regularly, and it was a reminder that helped her frame perspective to our pain.

Second, Rachel told me that I needed to help her create ways to remember our baby who died. There's a really good chance that your partner doesn't know how to help you in this desert season. I didn't know where to begin. It took Rachel telling me she wanted us to annually set up memorials to remember our child and this season of our life together. Tell your partner what would be meaningful to you. It's okay if he doesn't think of this on his own. I didn't. At first Rachel was disappointed and discouraged that I didn't do this on my own, which I totally understand. Thankfully, though, she brought me into this thought process and shared the idea with me. I'm so glad she took the initiative to do that with grace.

We input the dates to remember in our shared iPhone calendar—namely, our baby's due date and the anniversary of our loss. We did breakfast out on our baby's first due date; Rachel wanted to do something different from our standard morning routine, and I suggested she pick whatever felt right. Again, I wish I had brilliant ideas in my back pocket that were meaningful, but I simply didn't.

It was all new territory for me, and I relied a lot on listening to what she needed and then acting on it.

Lastly, let me encourage you to gracefully spell out your needs to your partner. There were countless days when Rachel and I were on completely different wavelengths in this journey of grief. I wasn't saying anything. I didn't know what to say. Or, to be frank, I just wasn't grieving as much because I thought I had already processed and moved on from the sorrow. My body wasn't still feeling the effects of the loss.

I remember Rachel telling me in our kitchen one night that she needed me to ask her questions about our lost child. She needed me to tell her what I was thinking and feeling about this desert season. Did I think our baby was a boy or a girl? What would I miss doing with him or her if they had grown up? It's not that I wasn't sad or didn't care about the situation. I really did. I was just experiencing it differently from Rachel, and in order to love and care for her, I needed her to tell me what she needed me to do. And here's the thing—*I wasn't even aware of that.* Thankfully she expressed this to me. Don't be afraid to clearly communicate these dynamics. A lack of communication doesn't mean that he doesn't care or isn't grieving. He does. And he wants to help. He just doesn't know what it's like to have a miscarriage.

Besides running marathons, up until that point in our marriage, Rachel and I understood and related to each other quite well. We always knew what the other was thinking. But this was our first true encounter in a lonely desert, and no amount of study on each other's love languages prepared us for that.

Modern secular culture has no ability to give purpose and meaning to disappointment and suffering. Though I didn't necessarily realize it in the moment, in hindsight, I now see that God was actually doing something in and through us in our silent desert of waiting. Our marriage became stronger because our communication path was forged. I learned things about Rachel that I thought I knew but really didn't. I became a better empathizer. My heart, longing, and gratitude grew for having kids. We learned how to grieve *together.* I became a better husband. I became a better father. I became a better pastor. I became a better human.

And my hope muscle got a lot stronger understanding that, yes, we were in a valley—but a valley placed between the mountains of Good Friday and Resurrection Sunday. Though the silence of Saturday always comes from the cries of Friday, it's the joyous shouts of Resurrection Sunday that always conclude the week.

Or should I say, begin the new week.

PART III

The Hope of Sunday

Stages of Hope:
Active Hope

ten

The Chapter That Changes Your Story

People used to tell me "he will redeem the time," and I would nod and agree, with the little seed of faith left in my broken heart. And now I tell others "he will redeem the time" with that little seed of faith rooted in resurrection, realized in my whole heart.

Tracy, loss mom

Hope is an odd thing. Hope seems to operate on its own unpredictable timetable. When death appears to have closed the curtain, hope shows up in a surprising encore. That's exactly how hope entered the scene for Mary Magdalene and the other Mary, as they walked into the final day of Holy Week.

I love how God chooses to resurrect hope in a *deeply* personal way. The first women to experience hope's rebirth were the same women who witnessed Jesus's murder on Friday. They were the same women who then watched Jesus's lifeless body be carried into the tomb. The women who possibly felt the greatest fear and hopelessness in the deafening silence of Saturday were now the first to encounter hope again.

And so it is with you, friend. Of everything that you've experienced in the arc of your pregnancy and your loss, you felt it all first. You felt it most. You were the first to hold the positive pregnancy stick and feel that rush of adrenaline as your heart began pounding with new expectations. And later, with such cruelty, you were the first to feel the life inside of you threatened. Nobody felt the pains of death in losing your baby like you felt in your body. Nobody knows just what it was like to walk through the processional of silence and grief after your baby died like you do. And nobody else knows the intangible sense of loss when not just your baby was miscarried but your hope was too.

Hope comes to the hopeless first. And hope comes when it is least expected.

My greatest fear in the Silent Saturday season of my miscarriage was that I would never feel actively hopeful about life again. I was scared my relationship with hope would never be the same, that it was too damaged to be repaired. I simply could not fathom holding hope again, the kind that allowed me to dream wild dreams and release my clenched fists of control.

And honestly, I can't pinpoint when I felt hope for the first time after my baby died. It wasn't during some noteworthy occasion where I got dressed up and left the house. It wasn't after a certain number of therapy sessions. Hope just began to appear again, unexpectedly yet slowly, not erasing grief but growing alongside it. It was as though hope really had been a seed planted in the darkness of silence and was beginning to grow.

I preface the resurrection of Jesus and the newfound sense of hope that comes with his defeat of death with all of this because it's important to avoid putting expectations on when you'll feel hopeful again after your baby dies. You will not have "feel hope today" written on a specific date in your calendar, as though it is a grief goal to reach. As loss moms, we live in the confusing tension of fearing hope and joy may wipe away the pain and existence of our babies' lives. It can be scary to hope again. After great loss, we have trust issues with hope. Once more, Jesus gets it.

When Hope Appeared

It was just another day of grieving for the two women named Mary when hope unexpectedly appeared on their radar. In fact, these two women were doing something most of us loss moms understand—they were visiting the place where their beloved was buried. What happened next would transform their hearts and the course of the world as we know it.

> After the Sabbath, at dawn on the first day of the week, Mary Magdalene and the other Mary went to look at the tomb. There was a violent earthquake, for an angel of the Lord came down from heaven and, going to the tomb, rolled back the stone and sat on it. His appearance was like lightning, his clothes were white as snow. . . . The angel said to the women, "Do not be afraid, for I know that you are looking for Jesus, who was crucified. He is not here; he has risen, just as he said." (Matt. 28:1–3, 5–6)

I imagine so much from this encounter must have shocked these grieving women—the earthquake, the angel audibly speaking to them, the stone rolling back from the tomb, and then their witnessing firsthand that the body of the one they loved was not inside. But what was likely most surprising to them was the angel's report that Jesus's body had not been stolen or gone missing. It had risen. Jesus had physically resurrected.

In the ancient world, people believed the resurrection would happen someday and that all of God's people would be resurrected together at one specific time. They had no expectation that *one* would be resurrected out in front of the rest of God's people, as a foretaste of what was to come. Furthermore, they had essentially lost all hope that Jesus was the Messiah—for they had no framework of a crucified Messiah. It was an oxymoron. A true Messiah wouldn't be subjected to such a humiliating, human death. But then someone who died a humiliating, human death wouldn't be physically resurrected from the dead, unless . . . could it be? Maybe Jesus really *was* the Messiah. Maybe they weren't hope-struck fools for believing he was the one to fulfill their hope all along. Maybe?

The angel told the women to go see it for themselves. "Head into Galilee and tell the rest of the disciples too" (28:7, my paraphrase).

How did the women feel in this moment? Matthew says they were "afraid yet filled with joy" (v. 8). This is the second explicit mention of fear in this scene and the biggest clue that Jesus knew—rather, expected—that those with hearts scarred by loss would be afraid to hope again.

Jesus didn't wait for the women to make it all the way to Galilee. I imagine he was like a child on Christmas, too excited to make them wait a second longer to open the gift of resurrection hope he carried. The story continues.

Suddenly Jesus met them. "'Greetings,' he said. They came to him, clasped his feet and worshiped him. Then Jesus said to them, 'Do not be afraid'" (vv. 9–10).

Jesus is so deeply aware of the fear that accompanies hope for those who have experienced deep loss. Not only is he aware, but he is amazingly sensitive to this reality. On the days when it feels scary to hope and easier to retreat into hopelessness, Jesus takes your hand and whispers the same words: *Do not be afraid of hope. I get it. I'm here.*

What Difference Does This Make?

I need to tell you something important. When people would tell me I didn't "need to be sad" after my baby had died "because [I'd] see my baby again," I was like, *Blah blah blah, that's great, but that doesn't change how much this hurts now.* What good was a future promise when it didn't touch my current reality?

Little did I know then how much the future promise was actually impacting my current reality. Knowing that this grand story my life is a part of will one day end in redemption drastically changed how I lived out the confusion in the middle of the plot. Without the implications of Jesus's resurrection, my loss and grief would have been much different. Here's what I mean.

I once heard a loss mom, who I gather doesn't follow Jesus, talk about how final death feels and how heavy that finality is. I paused, chewed on this, and kept moving. A few days later, I was still thinking about it—and here I am a year later writing about it. I so often forget that death feels absolutely final without the promise of Jesus's resurrection. If I didn't believe in Jesus, I would be living now without any active hope of seeing my baby again one day. If I didn't believe in Jesus, the few memories I had with my baby years ago would be all I'd ever have. And if I didn't believe in Jesus, I believe I'd be grieving *without* hope.

There are two different story lines available for life: one that shouts "this story ends in death" and another that whispers "this story ends with the defeat of death and the restoration of everything death has touched." One story ends with death. The other story ends with hope.

Maybe this is what the apostle Paul was getting at when he says we don't have to grieve like those without hope (1 Thess. 4:13). I always felt like it was just a verse people in the church said to grievers to politely encourage them to "cheer up." But I see Paul's point now. He's pointing us to the choice to align our grief with one of two story lines: death or hope. Those who don't know of or believe in Jesus and his defeat of death live in a world where death is final. They live in a world where miscarriage or stillbirth has had the last word in their baby's story.

But to know Jesus is to have hope as the final punctuation mark in your story, which shapes how you grieve in the messy middle. Does this hope minimize the pain of loss? Absolutely not. But resurrection hope promises this: Miscarriage does not get the last say in your baby's life. Stillbirth does not get to be the final verdict. Infant loss is not how your child's story ends. The hope of heaven, brought to life again through the risen Jesus, gets the last word.

And when hope has the last word in any story, it's going to be a story worth living, reading, and retelling.

New Creation

The resurrection of Jesus provides a foretaste of the full redemption we will experience in what the Bible calls the new heaven and new earth (Rev. 21), when the hope of heaven will become our full reality. Remember God's perfect design for humanity that he declared good and beautiful in Genesis and how he set into motion a plan to redeem the effects of sin? Jesus's resurrection is a deposit on God's promise. It's God's way of saying, "I'm going to make good on my promise to redeem all of creation—Jesus's resurrection is an appetizer to the main course of new creation ahead."

What will happen in the new creation? Physical bodies will experience resurrection. Death will be eradicated once and for all. I believe that the resurrection promise means one day we will hold our babies again, in full health and glory. Evil will be wiped out—for good. The foretaste of the resurrection will become the main course. And redemption will reign in full. Tim Keller puts it this way: "The Biblical view of things is resurrection—not a future that is just a consolation for the life we never had but a restoration of the life you always wanted. This means that every horrible thing that ever happened will not only be undone and repaired but will in some way make the eventual glory and joy even greater."[1]

Redemption

Redemption is one word that can set Christianity apart from all other religions. God isn't content just to say "I'll erase evil when this is all said and done," but in his deep and gracious mercy, God says, "I'm going a step further. Anywhere evil has left a fingerprint of death on your life, I'm redeeming that."

God's redemption is a theme that runs throughout Scripture. The word *redemption* in the first-century world literally meant to "buy back."[2] Redemption was the term for buying a slave back from the slave market and purchasing their freedom. The process of redeeming slaves—breaking actual chains and exchanging captivity to pain for freedom—so closely mirrors the way God breaks the chains of evil and death off humanity. He breaks the hardness off of broken hearts and the shame off our stories. Jesus, the Great Redeemer, comes to offer you hope and life in exchange for death.

You may wonder, *So, if all this is true, why is there so much evil in the world today?* And you're right to ask that question. We still live in the sin-fallen world of Genesis 3, as we await Jesus's return when he comes to usher in the new creation and set the world to rights once and for all. The new creation promises the ultimate culmination of God's redemption. But we don't have to wait for that glorious day when heaven comes to experience God's redemption. God is at work to bring healing and redemption right now.

Redemption after Loss

It can be tricky to navigate redemption after loss. There's a part of your heart that may desire God to bring something redemptive out of the ashes of your loss, while another part of your heart feels guilty for even desiring that. In this tension, we must remember that the hope and redemption Jesus offers does not gloss over, wipe out, or minimize your loss. Whatever Jesus can redeem from your loss in the future is also not "the reason why your baby died" or the "silver lining." Any redemptive healing you experience is simply the by-product of a God who loves his kids too much to leave evil untouched in their stories. He's big enough to bring something out of your deepest pains. And he loves you enough to do it.

The invitation to open your heart to the possibility of God's redemption after loss is hard. I won't sugarcoat that. The temptation is to sulk in pain, to not want to move out of it, and to not desire a different future. I've seen so many hurting moms allow pain to harden their hearts toward God, toward other moms with living babies, or toward the world around them in general. It's a heartbreaking and painful place to live. The invitation even amid grief is to open yourself up to the *possibility* of God's future redemption for your story.

Do you believe that God is capable of some redemptive healing in your story? You don't have to know *how* he'll bring beauty from ashes or even be ready for that yet. Like unclenching a white-knuckled fist, an openness to God's redemption is like saying,

"God, I'm scared to move forward with hope. I'm not sure how to unharden my heart, but I'm open to your redemption in my story."

No matter how dark or hopeless it seems your story is now, God's redemption is for *you*. How can I be sure? I've lived it.

A Redeemed Perspective

Redemption can sound so abstract until we pause to look back and see where God has redeemed parts of our stories. When I look back over my miscarriage, I consider the story below as one of the first tangible examples of God's redemption.

I was already seeing my therapist, Samantha, before my miscarriage happened. I had no idea that miscarriage also filled chapters of her story, and she became a true godsend in my grief. What I grew to really appreciate about Samantha was not only her ability to relate to my pain but also her choice to end our sessions with thought-provoking questions that often stung a bit to hear but slowly moved me to ask God what hope or redemption he may have had in store for my pain. It was a place I knew I needed to go, but looking beyond immediate pain can be scary. What if God wasn't going to do anything with all of this heartache? What if my dreams would remain shattered? What if redemption was for everyone else but me?

As my mind would race with these questions, I'd sink deeper into the armchair, and Samantha would lean closer, as though she could see the fears swirling in my brain. Therapists are good like that.

"Rachel." She paused. "What if you get the gift of a new perspective through all of this?"

"What kind of a new perspective?" I asked, doubtful but curious.

"After I lost my babies, I never saw motherhood the same way again. I never took lightly the gift of having children or raising them. Even on the hard days of raising my teenage girls now, the challenges are colored by this different perspective."

I was intrigued. Could there be something redemptive for me in all of this?

Samantha continued, "When I look at my friends who got pregnant on their first tries and never walked this path of loss that you and I share, sometimes I'm actually sad for them—because they'll never get this *gift* of a different perspective. When you've lost a baby, you see everything differently. It all becomes a miracle."

Deep in my heart, little flickers of hope fluttered around like butterflies in a nervous stomach. I resonated with what Samantha shared. I had already begun thinking differently about so many aspects of life and motherhood, and now, she had put words to my thoughts.

Something was shifting in my heart. Priorities were realigning. Dreams were gaining clarity. I was experiencing the type of new, redeemed perspective author Nicholas Wolterstorff describes after his son died: "I shall look at the world through tears. Perhaps I shall see things that dry-eyed I could not see."[3]

Losing the opportunity to be a mother made me realize just how deeply my heart held this dream. I *was* seeing everything differently. And this, I believe, was how I started to encounter God bringing something redemptive out of my pain. This was God turning one of the most sorrowful losses of my life into a key that unlocked a beautiful new perspective on life and motherhood that remains one of the most precious gifts God has given me through my baby's life and death. This did not bring my baby back, but I was starting to see some beauty arise from the smoldering ashes.

I could fill the rest of these pages with real-life stories of redemption from other loss moms. The way they've encountered hope, like the two women named Mary approaching Jesus's empty tomb, has been unexpected, often scary, and yet incredible.

I could tell you the story of how my sister-in-law Becka struggled with infertility for years before we gathered around her hospital bed, shedding tears of lament, as she lost her miracle baby, Rosalyn Hope, at seventeen weeks. We gathered around a similar hospital bed a year later, shedding tears of disbelief, as Becka birthed her living rainbow baby, Wilder Clement.

I could also tell you about how my friend Ashley has experienced newfound joy in serving other bereaved families in memory of her stillborn daughter, Parker.

Or I could tell you how I walked past that cold hospital bench where my miscarriage was confirmed, eleven months later, with a living son in my arms. The doctor who felt cold to me during my miscarriage now felt like a warm friend. I had trusted her to bring my new son into the world, and my once-blaming heart felt a bit more whole. As I buckled my baby into the car for the very first time, I looked back at that bench and felt a wink from God, as though he was personally reminding me that death did not have the last word.

But the most crucial thing I can tell you is that hope is not just for every other loss mom's story—it is for yours too. Hope comes to the hopeless, to the ordinary, to the grieving, to the ones who feel the good things come to everyone else but them. God's redemption is for *you*. And I want to help you open your grief-stricken heart to witnessing redemption in your story. It's time to head there now.

eleven

Stories without Pretty Bows

It may well be that, when all is said and done and our life stories are penned to their final paragraph, the thickest part of the plot was what we did with what was broken.

Beth Moore

I've loved stories since my elementary school days. I still have a crumpled piece of notebook paper my mom saved with a newscast outline I penciled around age seven, complete with all types of stories: the sad ones, the informative ones, and the happy ones. So, compelled by stories and their ability to inform us about humanity, I spent my undergraduate years studying journalism before entering a career as a professional storyteller. Why? Because stories teach us, stories inspire us, and stories connect us.

You know the movies you can't stop talking about? The books with plotlines that stick in your soul for years to come? Our culture has had an intrinsic gravitation toward stories since the beginning of history. Ever wonder why most of the Gospels involve Jesus telling parables (stories)? There's something innately powerful about stories.

But there are stories that *don't* make box-office records or get published. These are stories that don't follow the traditional, sensationalized, "Everyone is happy in the end" fairy-tale arc. These are the stories about *real* life, the ones where broken hearts, broken dreams, and broken people are the main characters. The ones where perfect hope seems like a fleeting theme, and for the foreseeable future, there are only chapters of grief or loss.

Living in a Broken Chapter

We've already talked about the hope of redemption at the end of each of our stories, which can plant hope on the horizon of every plotline, no matter how broken it seems. But I want to be very real with you about how we live out the chapters in between, the ones that don't make sense and the ones that can feel shameful to tell or even accept as part of your life's narrative.

When I was twenty-nine, I found myself living in a chapter I didn't know how to make sense of, and the world around me didn't want me to share. But this wasn't just any chapter—this one was deeply personal. The main character was my unborn baby who went to heaven before ever being held by human hands. This chapter was not on track with my life's plotline, and that not only hurt when I lived it but it also stung each time I witnessed the world around me not making space for other stories of loss like mine. As far as I knew, this chapter of my life didn't have a happy ending. I didn't know what would happen next. All I knew was that I didn't need to wait for my happy ending to start talking about my plot twist. And so that's what I did, and that's what I hope you can find permission to do with your baby loss story too.

I want to equip you the best I can to be a brave teller of your life's unexpected chapters—especially the one you're in now. The death of your baby is now and will forever be a significant part of your story, but it doesn't have to be an invisible chapter. Here are the three main challenges I've discovered for loss moms when it comes to sharing their stories and how to work through them.

1. We sanitize death

I didn't really want to go to the pregnancy and infant loss support group. My introverted side just wanted to spend Thursday night relaxing at home without any makeup on. When I finally did arrive, the couples introduced themselves and briefly shared their stories.

One woman began, "My name is Andrea, and my baby died twenty-four years ago."

Her husband piped in, "There's not a day we don't think about our daughter we lost."

"She died," Andrea shot back. "We didn't *lose* her—she's not missing. She's dead."

I could tell there was weighty importance packed into those words for Andrea. It wasn't merely a linguistic preference between loss and death. Those words to her—*loss* and *death*—had completely different meanings, and I understood her passion.

We live in a culture that sanitizes death. Most people aren't comfortable talking about death, grief, pain, or suffering (as you probably know firsthand by now). So, we resort to sanitizing death and using softer language. This may seem like a small nuance, but when death is part of your story after your baby dies, you are left in a confusing state of feeling the need to minimize what actually happened. When someone talks about losing something, it sounds casual. *Loss* doesn't stop your heart in its tracks the way *death* does. Death is no one's favorite word. Culture connects death with hopeless finality. Death sounds real and blunt, heavy and forceful; loss feels sanitized and slightly more comfortable. My baby died. He is dead. But of all the times I had talked about my miscarried baby up until that meeting, I had referred to him as the baby I lost, never my baby who died.

But now, thanks to Andrea, I try to make an intentional choice when I communicate the scope of my story. My baby isn't lost and missing, and his departure wasn't a peaceful passing. It was tragic and traumatic, like a thief trespassing in the night, forcefully robbing my body of my most prized possession with my hands tied defenseless. That's what I felt. That's what my story aches to declare. If I carry the weight of my baby's death, I can give myself permission to share the weight of this death with others. I am not responsible for any discomfort the "death" in my story makes others feel. To sanitize the death in my story is to rob it of its truth.

Furthermore, there are still some people who don't really think pregnancy loss or infant loss is real death. (I know, it sounds bizarre.) They believe these types of death impact a person less because the baby died in the womb, but as any loss mom knows, this does not minimize the loss we experience. When I say that my baby died, I am also subconsciously communicating that my baby *lived*. I am testifying to the reality that there was once life in my womb, because only what was alive can die. And sometimes, it's not just the world around me that doesn't understand pregnancy and infant loss that needs to hear that. Sometimes my heart needs the reminder of my baby's life and existence too.

Spiritually, for followers of Jesus, we can encounter a strange comfort that can be found when we acknowledge death. We can hold fast to the truth that after death comes resurrection, and what is true of Jesus's story will also be true of our stories. As a believer in the resurrected Jesus, when I mutter the dark word of death and acknowledge its place in my story, I'm simultaneously acknowledging the resurrection hope Jesus promises will follow. The resurrection is not a distant daydream, disconnected from your current reality. In fact, the resurrection very practically shapes how you tell your baby's story today and how this chapter fits into the larger story God is penning through your life.

2. We feel shame

Shame is one of the sneakiest challenges that will try to keep you from telling your story. It's sneaky in that it is often hard to pinpoint shame for what it is. Shame can mask itself in feeling embarrassed about your story, blaming yourself for your baby dying, or feeling like your baby dying is a heavy secret to keep hidden from your story, not integrated into it.

Sadly, the vast majority of loss moms feel shame surrounding their baby's death.

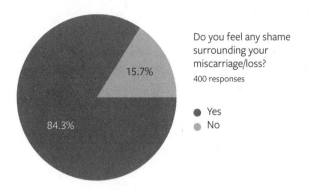

Do you feel any shame surrounding your miscarriage/loss?

400 responses

● Yes
● No

Of the loss moms I surveyed, these were the most common reasons they listed for feeling shame:

○ Feeling like my body failed
○ Feeling like my loss was my fault
○ Feeling like I could have prevented my loss
○ Feeling guilt for not knowing my pregnancy could end in loss
○ Feeling like I had no safe space to talk about my loss

As a loss mom, you have to be overly aware of how shame impacts your story and sense of self after your baby dies. You're up against the external forces of living in a culture that is silent toward pregnancy and infant loss, you may be in a family that doesn't talk about vulnerable parts of their stories, and you could even experience feeling unwelcome to share your story in your church (although I pray this is not the case for you). These influences are strong reinforcers of the shame many loss moms struggle with after their babies die.

When you are implicitly or explicitly told that a significant chapter of your life's story is unwelcome in the world, shame is the natural by-product. You start to internalize the implications of the world being uncomfortable with death, and soon lies of shame begin whispering into your identity: *There must be something wrong with me and my story. Nobody wants to hear it. It's too messy. Too uncomfortable. It makes other people too afraid of losing their babies.* When you feel like your story isn't welcome, like the 42 percent of loss moms who told me they felt they had no safe space to share their story, you start to feel unwelcome too. And what happens next? These external voices become the gateway for shame to take root. Here's how that happens.

Because questions loom and most of us never receive complete answers as to why our babies died, this chapter can be especially challenging to process. Our brains don't know how to make sense of the story.

Remember when you learned about the structure of stories in elementary school? They have three parts: a beginning, a middle, and an end. According to research cited in a fascinating article by neurologist Robert Burton, your brain actually rewards you with the chemical dopamine when it is able to recognize and complete patterns.[1] Stories are patterns. The brain recognizes the beginning-middle-end structure of a story and rewards you when you can clear up any ambiguity in that structure. It doesn't matter to the brain if what you fill in the gaps of the story with is actually truth. The brain doesn't fact-check. Thus, our default is to come up with a story that makes sense, feels familiar, and offers us insight into how to best self-protect against feeling the same pain again. It's a human survival instinct.

I saw how real this was when I witnessed a fellow loss mom process her baby's death. In an effort to make meaning of this terribly confusing chapter she was living in, she began finding familiar parts of her life narrative that aligned with her current experience. She fixated on everything she had lost in life and on the things she felt like God had withheld or taken from her. She soon found herself on a slippery slope, assuming the trajectory of her entire life narrative would always be something like this: Good things happen for everyone else but me.

In reality, this loss mom still had many good things in her life, but she had spiraled to a place where she could see only the chapters of her past and the chapters yet to be written through this lens of loss. Life was not going to improve for her, she would never have the good things everyone else did, and only more disappointment was on the horizon. Her brain went with what was familiar, completed the story pattern, and she began to believe it. As pastor Pete Hughes writes, "The story we live in is the story we live out."[2] And in this instance, as is so common for loss moms, shame moved into the story and spilled out into everyday life.

It took me a lot of introspection, prayer, and therapy to identify and then remove the shame that had sunk into my own heart when I tried to make sense of why my baby had died. I needed to sit with the truth that what happened to me—the death of my baby—did not happen *because* of me.

No matter the degree of shame you are carrying today, God desires to free you from every ounce of it. His redemption and healing applies to the shame-stained pages of your story just as much as it does to every other page. Will you grant yourself permission to be freed from any shame surrounding your baby's death?

I've found that simply praying a prayer like this has personally brought me healing from my shame, as well as many other loss moms I've led through it. If you're ready, open your hands in front of you and pray:

God, I surrender the pain of this chapter of my story to you today. I open my hands to any shame I may be holding on to and invite your healing to touch my story where shame has taken root. [Now, place your hands over your heart.] *Help my heart to believe the truth about who you say I am, not what shame has said. Thank you that I am loved, I am seen, and I am safe with you. Help me to trust in your hope today.* [Lastly, place your hands over your stomach.] *Today, in your presence, God, I forgive my body for any way I am blaming it for my baby's death. I forgive myself for any way I am blaming myself for my baby's death. I release any other person or thing I have been blaming for my baby's death. Help me to forgive today as you have forgiven me. Amen.*

3. We don't know how this chapter ends

"This is just not how my story was supposed to unfold," I confessed to my husband after our baby died. I couldn't get past the hang-up of this giant interruption in the plotline I had penciled into my life's story. The plot I had written for myself was predictable, like those stairsteps of life we talked about a few chapters back. Having children was the next chapter of my life, and we were right on time. Empty arms, a broken heart, and fractured dreams were not supposed to start this chapter, but now they did. And there was nothing I could do to rewrite the beginning. I couldn't erase the fact that loss was how my motherhood story would now *always* begin.

The third biggest challenge that looms in the face of telling your baby's story is that you're living in the middle of your story. How do you tell a story when you only know the beginning and middle but not the end? Your story has encountered dramatic unpredictability. Loss has a harsh way of reminding us that we aren't really in control of much of our stories to begin with, which can leave the future of our stories feeling unpredictable and vulnerable.

Author Jerry Sittser puts it this way:

> When reading a story, we stand outside the time sequence of the narrative as the plot progresses. If we wish, we can read the last chapter first to discover how it ends even before we learn how it begins. We don't have the same luxury in the case of our own story. The reason is simple enough—we are in the middle of it. We bear the imprint of the past, with no power to change it; we look to the future, with no power to control it. We are confined to the present, whether ideal or miserable.[3]

For a loss mom, being confined to the present and facing an unpredictable future often takes the shape of these daily questions: Will I be able to get pregnant again? How long will I have to wait to be pregnant again? Will my future pregnancies end in loss? Will my infertility treatments work? Should I be exploring adoption, fostering, or surrogacy?

When my husband and I start a new series on Netflix, he goes into research mode. We watch an episode or two, then he beelines to his laptop and spends an hour researching the historical facts and reading plot predictors. He says he does it because he's curious and wants to best understand the story line we'll be following, but it frustrates me, because in the course of his research, he'll "accidentally" find out how the story ends. Without me! He goes on ahead of me, fast-forwarding through the middle, skipping straight to the end. And I just want to watch episode by episode, letting the unpredictability of the story unfold in real time, allowing my mind to wander about the possibilities and what-ifs along the way.

But I struggle to *live* out my own story this way. I am like my husband when it comes to my story, pleading with God to give me a peek at the plot spoilers so I can settle back into predictability and prepare my heart for what lies ahead.

I did this. After my miscarriage, I begged God to give me signs if I'd be able to get pregnant again and deliver a living baby. Silence. That question was never answered when I was in the middle of my chapter. God was inviting me into healing and hope rediscovery, *independent* of how my motherhood journey would turn out. I wanted to fast-forward through my healing, chase the rainbow of another baby, and put all of my hope and healing in *that* basket. *If I can have a living baby, I'll be healed of all this pain*, I thought. *I'll be able to hope again*. Then *I'll be able to trust God and forgive the hurts of my miscarriage*.

But God does not operate on my commands. He was more concerned with the transformation of my heart. How was I allowing grief to shape my soul? How was loss changing me as a person? Was I willing to forgive those I blamed for my loss (including my body), even before I became pregnant again? Was I willing to draw close to God, the one who had been closest to me in my garden of grief and the silence of my Saturday, even if he didn't reveal in plain detail how hope would play out in my story?

Sitting in the middle of your story is a transformative space. This is where sacred soul work happens. Once more, Jerry Sittser shares, "Inner transformation could be—and often is—the real plot of the redemptive story."[4]

The Power of a Broken Story

Friend, you have permission today to talk about your motherhood journey even if you don't have a pretty bow to tie around it. You have permission to just be in the messy middle of your story, awaiting redemption, yet encountering transformation. *That* is a story to tell.

Actually, more people are living this type of story than you realize. They're just not the stories our culture sensationalizes, so we shy away from telling them ourselves. But these are the best stories. They are the real, gritty stories of God's redemption meeting broken hearts where they hurt most. These are the stories of transformation, where the mysterious exchange of ashes for beauty and shame for grace is being written right before our eyes. These are the stories that connect us, free us, and point us to hope.

When you tell *that* part of your story—when you talk about your storm even before you see the rainbow after the clouds clear—you are showing others in real time what it is like to courageously walk the bumpy road to hope again. And you're granting them permission to do the same.

twelve

Touching Hope in the Scars

The tears hit the pillow tonight, punctuating the silent confusion of why I was overcome with this unexpected wave of grief today. Each drop on the pillow felt significant. The first one hit—validating my body's inner sadness now expressed, safely, with permission to come out. Then there was another tear; I think my count stopped around five in total. Five punctuations of the silence. And then I remembered this is different from May 28, 2017. On that day, the punctuations were flipped. The wailing tears were the constant, punctuated by rare moments of silence as I would inhale deeply to catch my breath. There were tears in abundance and silence in drops. And with each year, that rhythmic balance has changed. The silence has grown. The tears have decreased. But they still exist in a dynamic dance together as my body begs me not to forget a central piece of its story.

my journal entry, May 28, 2022
(the five-year anniversary of my baby's death)

In 2018, a female orca named Tahlequah made headlines. Killer whales don't usually make headlines, but she did. Tahlequah became famous for carrying the body of her dead calf for seventeen straight days, nudging it toward the surface of the Pacific Ocean near the coast of the Pacific Northwest and Canada. For more than two weeks, this grieving mother did not let her baby's corpse drift to the ocean floor. She kept her baby afloat right next to her as she swam, as though she was intentionally integrating her baby's life into her life, even after death. One oceanic expert is quoted in an article about Tahlequah, noting, "This kind of behavior is like a period of mourning and has been seen before. What's extraordinary about this is the length of time."[1]

It must have been extraordinary to watch a mourning killer whale carry her dead baby for seventeen days. But as a loss mom, you know firsthand that even seventeen days is no extraordinary time at all when it comes to preserving the memory of your baby. Just as you'll never be done grieving your baby's death, you'll never stop carrying the memory of your baby's life. With time, you'll begin integrating your baby's life and memory into *your* life.

We've looked at the unique set of challenges we face as loss moms to both grieve and keep our babies' stories alive in a culture that is largely silent on pregnancy and infant loss. And we've also explored how to grieve in healthy ways and how to work through the confusing middle of our stories when we can't see the specifics of what lies ahead.

By no choice of your own, you are now the owner of a very powerful story. You've experienced the expectations of new life, the crushing disappointment of your baby dying, the silence of grief, and you're still here. You've survived a soul-crushing devastation, and you're alive to talk about it. You are the owner of a very powerful story. Like Tahlequah, it's time to look at how to integrate your baby's memory into your life. It's time to see why the very powerful story you own needs to be told.

Your Story as Memorial

Author Zoë Clark-Coates says, "When a parent loses a baby, their final act of love is keeping their story alive."[2] This is another beautiful invitation to view your grief as love. What if you framed this painful chapter of loss in your story as a living memorial, an ongoing tribute to your baby? This may feel counterintuitive in a culture that says to keep the painful parts of your story hidden, but I know how much your heart is aching to keep your baby's memory alive.

The temptation will always be to hide the vulnerable parts of your story, to convince yourself your painful chapters are safer when they are kept out of sight. But when you silo a significant part of your story off to the side, which may be more comfortable initially, you can create long-term barriers to your grief and healing. The hidden parts of your story can also become pieces of life to idealize—always wanting to return back to—or to regret, like a tape that replays over and over, while you imagine what you could've done differently.[3] For a loss mom, the endless cycle of mental what-ifs and "if I had another chance . . ." can become a prison over time, holding both your story and your healing captive.

I invite you to pause and ask yourself, *How am I attempting to silo or dismiss this chapter of my story?* And instead ask, *How can I authentically seek to integrate my loss into my story?* Jerry Sittser says that as grievers, we have an invitation to remember the past as "redemptive memory"—not as an idealized part of our stories to which we are always wanting to return, or as a giant regret we wish to go back and change, "but as one chapter in a larger redemptive story we continue to live out in the present moment."[4] Living with hands tied to the past is actually saying, "I believe my only memories with my baby are the ones I've already had," and in essence, implies resurrection does *not* apply to our stories. Living with *active* hope remembers the past in a way that anticipates redemption ahead and sounds more like "I love and miss my baby so much. I am filled with curiosity about his/her life. I can't wait to see him/her again."

The next time you're nervous or hesitant to include your baby's death when you tell your story, reframe this chapter in your mind. It is not a shameful chapter that should remain hidden for fear of making others too uncomfortable. Rather, it is a chapter about your baby, your child, your own flesh and blood, and telling this chapter as part of your story is an active memorial of love to your baby.

Your Story as Healing

The first time I publicly talked about my miscarriage, everything I was hoping to avoid happened. My voice shook, I cried, I couldn't finish my sentences, and afterward, a woman rudely suggested that my baby dying was my fault. But this would not derail me from telling my story again; in fact, it was only the first of hundreds of times I would go on to tell my story. Looking back, it was the first seed planted for an online community of loss moms to share their stories that would be birthed years later.

Even when telling my story means things like voice crackings and unwelcome comments, I won't stop telling it. Why? Telling my story has been one of the most healing experiences in my grief journey. Maya Angelou famously said, "There is no greater agony than bearing an untold story inside you."[5] Living life day after day with an untold story is a heavy load to shoulder. And the very first time I told my story, I felt the weight of that load lessen a bit. It was like I was finally being honest with the people around me and being honest with myself. I was broken, I was hurting, and I was the owner of an imperfect yet very powerful story, one that was encountering God's redemption before my eyes.

We are made for connection and wired for story. When you share your story, you come out of hiding. You encounter healing in a bold, vulnerable way. Many of the women who share their stories with me through Hope Again Collective are sharing it for the first time. And when they see their story posted and reshare it with their own networks, they articulate a new sense of empowerment. They've come out of hiding. They've embraced the parts of their story that the world around them has told them to hide. They've encountered healing.

On sharing her story, a loss mom named Liesl writes: "Having a safe space to talk about the impact of my son's life and death has made a big difference and gives me hope. For me, sharing my story is part of my healing journey."

Your Story as Connection

Of the moms I surveyed, the most common fears they felt around sharing their infant loss stories were feeling misunderstood, others thinking they wanted attention, or receiving pity. But by far, the *largest* fear loss moms have when sharing their story is being judged by others.

With those fears in mind, consider these scenarios. What happens when a close friend shares the hard chapters of their life with you? How do you feel when a stranger is giving a speech, a message, or a TED Talk, and they share honestly about their own brokenness? I usually want to hear *more*. I find myself instantly respecting and connecting with the person sharing. They've just shown me an honest, vulnerable peek into their pain.

Why am I inclined to respect a story and honor the storyteller's pain, rather than judge them? Because brokenness connects us. This is not a coincidence, and it is not dependent upon the storyteller. Deep within all of our narratives are hidden chapters revealing our deepest brokenness. Pain is a shared human experience. Most of us suffer in silence, shame, or secrecy. When someone is brave enough to step out of the stigma and broach the elephant-in-the-room of pain, listeners breathe a collective breath of relief and comfort.

When we share our scars, we show people they are not alone in their pain. Pain can be an extremely powerful tool for connecting with just about anyone. We all have it, but most of us never talk about it. What if sharing your brokenness could actually free someone to embrace their own?

Your Story as Stigma Changing

"I was so nervous to share my story because of the stigma around infant loss. A dear friend told me if I could touch at least one person, then it would be worth doing. She was right." This is what a fellow loss mom named Tocarra sent me after sharing the story of her twin girls: one stillborn, one born alive.

I believe the *primary* way the shame stigma surrounding pregnancy and infant loss will change is through loss moms courageously sharing their stories. I'm already witnessing it happening. When we share our stories, we normalize infant loss. We attest to the reality of the statistic: loss happens in one in four pregnancies. The statistic is a reality for millions of women, and not because we have broken bodies, some unforgivable sin in the past we are being "punished" for, or for any other absurd reason our culture may attribute to pregnancy and infant loss. Death happens. Loss happens. It's a by-product of living in a broken world, awaiting the fullness of heaven's death-defeating reign.

As a loss mom, you have a real gift to offer the world, and that gift is your story. You are a resilient woman with an imperfect story line, who has encountered real hope. As my dear friend Jacey, who has experienced multiple losses, writes,

> I'll meet those babies one day and it will be glorious. Until then, I'll keep sharing my story and continue to make it known that miscarriage may happen in one in four pregnancies. But the explanation through statistics will always leave a void when we look at it with kingdom eyes. I choose to feel the grief. I also choose to declare that miscarriage was not my fault, not my choice, but always will be the story of how I was able to know my maker a little bit more deeply.

On the days when you feel like nobody in your life cares about your story, remember that Jesus does; in fact, he cares deeply about your story. How can I be sure? Jesus flocked to the same types of people during his ministry. Jesus went to the marginalized, to those with stories that had been shamed or silenced by culture at large, pushed aside, and left in the margins. Jesus cared then and he cares now about the stories and lives culture minimizes. He's in the front row each time you share your story.

Your Story as New Identity

"If someone asks, 'Who are you, tell me about yourself,' I say—not immediately, but shortly—'I am one who lost a son.' That loss determines my identity; not all of my identity, but much of it. It belongs within my story."[6] This is how author Nicholas Wolterstorff describes the integration of his son's death into his new identity.

You're not the same person you were before your baby died. And your story testifies to your new identity—how loss, grief, and hope have changed you. I've spent a lot of time reflecting on how loss has changed me and that included taking the time to mourn the parts of myself I lost when my baby died. I asked other loss moms how they've personally been changed through infant loss, then I used their responses to write a collective letter to my pre-loss self. As a tool to help identify, grieve, and celebrate the ways loss has changed you, I invite you to do the same. Here's a portion of my letter.

> *Dear pre-loss self,*
>
> *After your baby dies, you are going to be a different person. An element of your naivety, innocence, and optimism will die too. It will be okay to miss these things and to miss the person you were before your baby died. You're going to see the world differently after your baby dies. The miracle of life itself, the pain others carry, the hope of a sunrise, the fragility of your existence, the flickers of redemption around you— these aren't visible on your radar now. But after loss, they'll be part of the way you see everything. There's a deep well of strength and resilience in you already; you don't know the depth of it yet. You're going to get through this. This will be a chapter of your story but not the end of your story.*

Anytime someone submits their story on my website, one of the last questions they answer is, How has your loss shaped you as a woman? These are my favorite responses to read. They are incredibly inspiring. Most women say loss has made them more empathetic, more comfortable sitting in the pain of others, more courageous to talk about loss, and more honest about their emotions. A lot of loss moms also articulate a new appreciation for the fragility of life, a renewed sense of gratitude for the miracles around them each day, and a vow to not take them for granted.

I love how one loss mom named Jana reflected on how loss changed her:

> Just yesterday I was telling a friend [that] I missed the girl I was before Jaxson. This friend challenged me that while losing Jaxson has taken me through something that made me darker and harder in some ways, it also created an empathy in me I didn't have before. She remembers the younger me being more legalistic, pious, and certain I was right about everything. Loss reduces your certainty and breaks the parts of yourself you lord over other people without realizing it. I want to be the person who says, "I've walked through the hardest thing anyone can walk through—and I've made it to some sunshine."

Your Story as Hope Giving

Friend, just like Jana, you have walked through the hardest thing anyone can walk through and you've made it to some sunshine. Do you recognize the hope your life testifies of? Your story is now a conduit of hope. Your story now contains the gift that so many other loss moms need to hear: Death will not have the last word of their story. Hope will. And *you* are living proof.

Last Christmas I named a holiday-themed earring after a loss mom named Chelsi. Her daughter Rosie Mae was born still. Chelsi reflected on the impact other loss mom stories had on her own hope journey: "I haven't had enough time to start feeling hopeful again, but hearing other women's stories reminds me that I'm not alone."

Probably a quarter of the DMs I receive echo this sentiment. They are loss moms telling me firsthand that reading the loss mom stories on my page is what has given them hope for their own grief journeys. Your family, friends, or Google may give you "advice" on finding hope after your loss, but there is something so different about hearing hope from a woman who has been in your shoes and knows firsthand the pain of a baby dying.

Do you realize the gospel message is reflected in your story? There is creation—everything good, as God intended; followed by the fall—brokenness, broken dreams, broken bodies, broken hearts; and then there is redemption—the new hope of resurrection. Your story has the power to point someone else to the saving hope of Jesus Christ. You will not know the gift of hope your story may give someone else until you share it. The probability is high that sharing your story will help another loss mom find hope for herself, and that gift can change everything.

Your Story for Hard Days

Telling your story is also for you. There will be hard days ahead in your grief journey, days when you need the reminder that you've survived all of your hardest days in the past, and God has not left you.

On the five-year anniversary of my miscarriage, the grief hit me unexpectedly hard. I turned the pages back in my journal that weekend and reread the chapter of my miscarriage—my own personal story of God walking with me as I rediscovered hope after loss. Sometimes the person who needs to hear your story the most is you. The hope in your heart needs to remind the fear in your head that the creator of the universe is kneeling beside you in the garden when your soul is crushed in anguish. He walks beside you through the betrayal of those who don't understand the scope of your loss, knows what it feels like to be alone, sits with you in the silence, and travels with you on the road to hope again.

God cares a lot about remembering. Among the largest themes of the Old Testament is remembering. God repeatedly tells Israel to remember how he provided for them in the desert. And one of the largest themes of the New Testament is also remembering. During the last meal Jesus eats before his body meets death, he says, "Whenever you break bread and drink wine again, remember me" (1 Cor. 11:24–25, my paraphrase). This is not God stroking his own ego. This is God providing his people with a demonstration of the spiritual practice of remembering his faithfulness.

When you remember God's faithfulness—how he walked *with* you during the hardest days of your past and did not allow death to be the last word of your story—it becomes the grounds for your faith to face the future. You can brave the uncertainty of future chapters knowing the one who has sustained you in the past promises to sustain you in the unknowns of the future. And there are *a lot* of unknowns in any motherhood journey. Whatever you face ahead, if your hope is placed in any factor, circumstance, or outcome, it will not be a hope sturdy enough to sustain you. The hope you've found in Jesus, the author and redeemer of your story, is the *only* hope strong enough to weather any storms of the future.

Still Doubting

There's one more thing that happens on the road to hope again, and it's important to tuck it in your pocket and keep with you.

On the same Sunday the resurrected Jesus appeared to the two women named Mary, he appeared to the disciples.

Jesus came and stood among them that evening and said, "'Peace be with you!' After he said this, he showed them his hands and side" (John 20:19–20).

Did you catch the significance of this? Jesus greeted them (the very first time he saw his loved ones after he was presumed dead), then he immediately did something that can radically change how you view your story: *he showed his scars.*

Pastor Ian Simkins shares the implications of this act: "After the resurrection Jesus showed his wounds. Maybe we don't have to hide ours either."[7] Let that sink into your heart and into your story.

A disciple named Thomas was absent the first time Jesus appeared and showed the disciples his scars, so when Thomas received the news about a resurrected Jesus, he had his doubts. He had his fears. *This whole hope after death thing*, he wondered, *is it too good to be true?* So, Thomas declared, "Unless I see the nail marks in his hands and put my finger where the nails were, and put my hand into his side, I will not believe" (20:25).

Friend, if you have made it this far in this book and still have your doubts that Jesus's redemption and resurrection hope is for *you*, you are not the first one to struggle to believe in resurrected hope. Having trust issues with hope, like Thomas did, is a normal reality of life after loss.

And it does not take Jesus by surprise. He is not disappointed that your road to hope has taken longer than another loss mom's journey, nor does he skip over you. Instead, he is willing to meet you right where you're at. What happens to Thomas next is proof:

> A week later his disciples were in the house again, and Thomas was with them. Though the doors were locked, Jesus came and stood among them and said, "Peace be with you!" Then he said to Thomas, "Put your finger here; see my hands. Reach out your hand and put it into my side. Stop doubting and believe." (20:26–27)

Touch the hope, says Jesus.

Active Hope

I thought I had hope before my baby died. But I had confused hope with a predictable story and a comfortable faith. It was only after I miscarried my hope that I truly found it. After loss, I found resurrected hope—an active, real, transformative, story-changing sort of hope. This is a hope that has changed my story, a hope that erased *death* as the final word of my baby's story. Finding resurrected hope through Jesus continues to be the greatest gift my baby has given me. I wouldn't have the active hope I live with today without my baby's life and death pushing me to the feet of resurrected Jesus.

Friend, I want to personally thank you for opening your heart to the possibility that your miscarried hope could be resurrected too.

On the days ahead when hope feels hard to locate, remember that resurrected hope has already been tested. It has already battled death, two thousand years ago on a wooden Roman cross. In the silence that followed, hope appeared defeated, but unexpected as it always is, hope had the last word. Hope won then, and hope wins today. Could it be that the road map for grief, healing, and hope after pregnancy and infant loss was already written over two thousand years ago? I think so.

Hope has a name, and his name is Jesus. And with resurrected hope in your scarred heart, you can face whatever uncertainties lie ahead in your story. Just as a mother cannot forget her child, this hope named Jesus will never forget you—or your baby.

Additional Resources

God's Truths for You on Hard Days

God has not and will not leave me. (Deut. 31:8)

God is with me wherever I go. (Josh. 1:9)

God is with me in my darkest moments. (Ps. 23:4)

God is close to me in my grief. (Ps. 34:18)

God hears my cries and prayers. (Ps. 66:17–20)

God promises to redeem my story. (Ps. 107:2)

God has compassion for me. (Ps. 145:9)

God is my strength when I feel weak. (Isa. 40:29)

God promises to be with me in my trials. (Isa. 43:2)

God has not and will not forget me. (Isa. 49:15–16)

God is a safe refuge for me in times of hardship. (Nah. 1:7)

God knows just what I need. (Matt. 6:31–33)

God gives rest to my weary soul. (Matt. 11:28–30)

Texts and Phrases to Support a Loss Mom

"I'm so sorry this happened."

"I'm thinking of you today. No need to reply."

"Your baby is loved."

"This is so unfair."

"This is not your fault."

"You did nothing wrong."

"You're doing your best."

"One day at a time."

"You're still a mom."

"Your baby's life matters."

"Your baby will not be forgotten."

"Would you like me to call your baby by a certain name?"

"What's a sweet memory you shared with your baby during pregnancy?"

"I love you as much as I always have."

"I'm not going anywhere."

"I'm here to listen."

Unhelpful Phrases to Avoid

"Everything happens for a reason."

"At least you know you can get pregnant" (or anything starting with "at least").

"You're young. You still have time."

"You can try again."

"You'll be pregnant again in no time."

Practical Ways to Care for a Mom after Her Baby Dies

Leave a homemade meal on her doorstep.

Have her favorite food delivered.

If she has living children, offer to babysit.

Pray for her regularly.

Send her a Scripture you've prayed over her.

Send her an e-gift card for food or coffee.

Give her a meaningful gift to remember her baby (jewelry, a journal, a tree to plant, a candle).

Treat her to some self-care (a gift card to a spa, nail salon, or massage appointment, etc.).

Bring her a special drink. ("I'm going to Starbucks. What can I bring you?")

Help her skip a trip to the grocery store. ("I'm going to the grocery. What can I pick up for you?")

Take something off her to-do list. ("I have some free time this week. Is there a day I could come clean your house/help with your laundry/run an errand for you?")

Invite her out with you. ("When are some good days I could pick you up for coffee/brunch/lunch/drinks/dinner?")

Gift her a Christmas ornament with her baby's name on it.

Send her a "thinking of you" card or a text on Mother's Day.

Put the date of her baby's death on your calendar and send her a card, text, or small gift on that day.

Light a candle in memory of her baby on October 15 and send her a photo. (Bereaved parents across the world honor their babies on this day during "Wave of Light.")

Check in weeks and months after her baby has died.

Things Loss Moms Wish the World Knew about Infant Loss

"It can happen to anyone at any time."

"It feels like a rug being pulled out from under you."

"It changes you forever."

"My baby did live."

"My child is real."

"Grieving the loss of your baby doesn't have an end date."

"It feels like a dream/hope/wish/future is taken away from you in a single moment and there's nothing you can do about it."

"It's like missing a part of yourself."

"It's unimaginable pain."

"You never move on from losing your child, but you do move forward."

"It's a devastation like no other. . . . Birthing and burying a dead baby is gut-wrenching and traumatic."

"I wish the healthcare system was more sympathetic."

"We want our babies remembered."

"Infant loss shouldn't be such an isolating experience."

"Ask and listen and share. Our stories matter."

"Miscarriage is the hardest thing I've ever experienced in my life."

"You don't just mourn the loss of your baby; you mourn the memories you were going to make with them."

"It's lonely. Please don't abandon us—we need support."

"This topic should not be silenced anymore."

Acknowledgments

This book began eleven years ago. When I was twenty-four, my pursuit of writing became serious. I had no idea then that my first published work would be fruit of such deep loss years later. There are so many special people who have helped water this seed of a writing dream for the past eleven years, and my heart swells with gratitude for the unique, God-positioned roles they've played in helping this seed spring up into something beautiful.

Bev Nault—you were the only author I knew in real life when I was a young twentysomething with writing ambitions. Thank you for taking me under your wing.

Renee Fisher—as we often joke, we've shared so many seasons of life together: singleness, dating, marriage, miscarriage, seminary, writing, entrepreneurship, and motherhood. The email from you that landed in my inbox in the spring of 2019 is what led to me picking this dream back up, putting pen to paper, and ultimately led to this book becoming reality. I hope you know the kingdom fruit you've yielded by way of encouraging the dreams of others. I'm so thankful for you.

To my agent, Karen Neumair—I'm still humbled you took me on over a decade ago and that you stayed the course with me through shifting writing ideas and unfolding life events. In this wild process, you've been a warm hand of wisdom to hold. Thank you.

Rachel McRae—I'm so thankful for your "yes." Thank you for seeing the ache of loss moms and for caring to help resource it. You've been everything I hoped for in an editor and more. Thank you for shepherding me not only as an author but also as a human being, for sharing a name with me, and for loving all things British! To everyone I've had the honor of learning from at Baker/Revell, I'm so thankful for your expertise, your kind guidance, and your enthusiasm over the course of this project. A special thank-you to Robin for lending your impeccable editing skills to this manuscript.

Kaitlyn Moore—thank you for all you do behind the screens to help me. I love learning from you, brainstorming with you, and calling you a friend.

Samantha—you hold the sacred space of being the first woman I knew who also experienced miscarriage. Your office was my primary place of processing life after my baby died. Thank you for the gift of a new perspective on motherhood and for leading me back to the tender arms of Jesus in my grief.

Tracy Brown—thank you for being you and for giving yourself so generously to support this idea. That Zoom call was the launching point I didn't know how much I needed. You're such a special person.

Becka Applegate—thank you for being an idea bouncer from the initial stages of Hope Again Collective and this book. While I wish we didn't have any babies in heaven, I'm thankful for our honest conversations about faith, grief, and stories that sometimes don't make sense.

Jacey Biermann, Andrea Burgess, Renee Fisher, Keri Larned, and Linda Williams—thank you for being my prayer covering. You are women of faith I admire and am blessed to call my friends. Thank you for the heavy spiritual lifting you did in interceding for this book during each phase of the process. I am so thankful for you!

To my parents—among all of the wonderful things you've done for me in life, three lessons in particular helped me write this book: (1) you encouraged me to dream and to dream big, (2) you taught me to make bold asks because "the worst they can say is no," and (3) you modeled a work ethic worthy of imitation. I love you, Mommy and Daddy!

To my siblings—I hate that we share this pain of knowing what it is to lose a baby. Yet in some way, it feels like another beautiful cord born out of hardship that knits us together. I love you both so much.

To Popsi—thank you for being my hero.

To any woman who has shared her story with me—thank you for allowing me to sit with you in that sacred space. I learn from you each day and do not take lightly the honor of holding some of the most vulnerable chapters of your story with you. Your bravery in sharing your experience with loss is the foundation of this book.

To anyone who has supported Hope Again Collective—thank you for caring about the experiences of moms who have lost their babies and for giving us the invaluable gift of finding hope again.

To Parker and Eden—I still can't believe I get to be your mom. Parker, it was through your pregnancy that I learned to trust God again. Eden, it was through your pregnancy that I learned to celebrate with God again. You have no idea the gifts you've given me by your mere existence. You're my favorite part of every day. I love you both.

To my husband, Mark—your brilliance is infused in these pages. You've helped me see Jesus and the story of Scripture with fresh eyes. Thank you for being my late-night sounding board on days of writing frustration and for telling me when to take a break, when to push through the blocks, and when to pack my bags to write a few chapters in Europe (talk about wisdom!). I hate that our parenthood began with tragedy, yet I wouldn't change how God has used the pain of never knowing our first baby to knit us closer into greater honesty and into a more intimate faith and for the way it has given us a parenting perspective with an eye on eternity. To share so many spheres of life with someone I admire, I learn from, and I laugh with is the greatest gift. I love you. (Now let's get your book written!)

To Jesus—thank you for loving me enough to meet me in my darkest hour of miscarriage. Journeying with you through loss changed our relationship—well, you've changed *everything* in my life. You are the hope. The redeemer of my story. And if this book draws just one person closer to you, it's been worth writing.

Notes

Chapter 1 A Two-Thousand-Year-Old Road Map

1. Timothy Keller, *Walking with God through Pain and Suffering* (New York: Penguin Books, 2015), 86.

2. The Miscarried Hope Survey, conducted electronically in May 2022, anonymously surveyed four hundred moms who have experienced miscarriage, stillbirth, or both. Quotes and information gathered from this survey are used throughout the book.

Chapter 2 Great Expectations

1. Grant R. Osborne, *Zondervan Exegetical Commentary on the New Testament: Matthew* (Grand Rapids: Zondervan, 2010), 756.

2. N. T. Wright, *Luke for Everyone* (Louisville: Westminster John Knox, 2004), 230.

Chapter 3 The Shock of a Supper

1. Carla Dugas and Valori H. Slane, "Miscarriage," National Library of Medicine, Stat Pearls, last updated June 27, 2022, https://www.ncbi.nlm.nih.gov/books/NBK532992/.

2. Brené Brown, *Atlas of the Heart* (New York: Random House, 2021), 91.

3. Brown, *Atlas of the Heart*, 91.

Chapter 4 Friends Who Fell Asleep

1. Merriam-Webster, s.v. "betray," accessed February 15, 2023, https://www.merriam-webster.com/dictionary/betray.

2. Brianna Leiendecker, "Empathy, Not Advice," in *Trauma in America*, Barna Group (Philadelphia: American Bible Society, 2020), 103.

Chapter 5 White Sheets

1. Timothy Keller, *The Reason for God* (New York: Riverhead Books, 2008), 29.
2. Keller, *Reason for God*, 29–30.
3. Jeffry Zurheide, *When Faith Is Tested* (Minneapolis: Fortress, 1997), 38.
4. Jerry Sittser, *A Grace Disguised* (Grand Rapids: Zondervan, 1995, 2004), 159.

Chapter 6 A Silent Culture

1. Peter Scazzero, *Emotionally Healthy Spirituality* (Grand Rapids: Zondervan, 2006), 145.
2. AJ Sherrill, *Being with God* (Grand Rapids: Brazos, 2021), 58.
3. Quoted in Brown, *Atlas of the Heart*, 102.

Chapter 7 Planting Seeds and Tearing Fabric

1. Anderson Herbert and Kenneth R. Mitchell, *All Our Losses, All Our Griefs* (Philadelphia: Westminster, 1983), 55.
2. Brown, *Atlas of the Heart*, 110.
3. Jerry Sittser, *A Grace Disguised*, 39, 44, 61, (cf. p. 37) as seen in *Emotionally Healthy Spirituality Day by Day* by Peter Scazzero (Grand Rapids: Zondervan, 2008), 101.
4. Elisabeth Kübler-Ross, *Death* (New York: Touchstone, 1986), 96.
5. Jerry Sittser, *A Grace Revealed* (Grand Rapids: Zondervan, 2012), 112.
6. Zalman Goldstein, "Kriah—Rending the Garments," Chabad.org, accessed August 2, 2022, https://www.chabad.org/library/article_cdo/aid/368089/jewish/Kriah-Rending-the-Garments.htm.
7. Timothy Keller, *Encounters with Jesus* (New York: Riverhead Books, 2013), 43.
8. Justin McRoberts, Twitter post, December 30, 2021, 8:49 a.m., https://twitter.com/justinmcroberts/status/1476596286946099202.

Chapter 8 The Three-Letter Question

1. Adriel Booker, *Grace Like Scarlett* (Grand Rapids: Baker Books, 2018), 44.
2. Zurheide, *When Faith Is Tested*, 20–24.
3. Zurheide, *When Faith Is Tested*, 22.
4. Scazzero, *Emotionally Healthy Spirituality*, 143.

Chapter 10 The Chapter That Changes Your Story

1. Keller, *Reason for God*, 32.
2. N. T. Wright, *Galatians* (Grand Rapids: Eerdmans, 2021), 208.
3. Nicholas Wolterstorff, *Lament for a Son* (Grand Rapids: Eerdmans, 1987), 26.

Chapter 11 Stories without Pretty Bows

1. Robert Burton, "Our Brains Tell Stories So We Can Live," Nautilus, August 6, 2019, https://nautil.us/our-brains-tell-stories-so-we-can-live-8377/.
2. Pete Hughes, *All Things New* (Colorado Springs: David C Cook, 2020), 323.

3. Sittser, *A Grace Revealed*, 104–5.

4. Sittser, *A Grace Revealed*, 120.

Chapter 12 Touching Hope in the Scars

1. CNN Wire, "Mourning Orca Whale Swims with Dead Body of Her Calf for More Than Two Weeks Off Coast of Northwest U.S., Canada," KTLA, August 10, 2018, https://ktla.com/news/nationworld/mourning-orca-whale-swims-with-dead-body-of-her-calf-for-more-than-two-weeks-off-coast-of-northwest-u-s-canada/.

2. Zoë Clark-Coates, Facebook post, May 22, 2022, 7:58 a.m., https://www.facebook.com/photo.php?fbid=495128802402620&set=pb.100057165142119.-2207520000..&type=3.

3. Sittser, *A Grace Revealed*, 161.

4. Sittser, *A Grace Revealed*, 161.

5. Maya Angelou, BrainyQuote.com, accessed January 19, 2023, https://www.brainyquote.com/quotes/maya_angelou_133956.

6. Wolterstorff, *Lament for a Son*, 6.

7. Ian Simkins, "#easter #resurrection," Instagram post, April 17, 2022, https://www.instagram.com/p/CceZVlMM91_/.

Rachel Lohman holds a master's degree in theology and ministry from Fuller Theological Seminary. She is a pastor, speaker, and founder of Hope Again Collective, a handmade jewelry line that shares the stories of loss moms. Rachel is a mother to two living children and one in heaven. She and her husband, Mark, currently lead The Bridge, a bilingual church in Southern California.

Connect with Rachel

at RachelLohman.com or online at:

@Rachel.Lohman and @HopeAgainCollective

@HopeAgainCollective